# YOUNG, RICH,
## AND DANGEROUS

## ALSO BY SAMANTHA MARSHALL

*Make It Happen: The Hip-Hop Generation Guide to Success* with Kevin Liles

# YOUNG, RICH, AND DANGEROUS

## THE MAKING OF A MUSIC MOGUL

# JERMAINE DUPRI

### with SAMANTHA MARSHALL

**ATRIA** BOOKS

NEW YORK   LONDON   TORONTO   SYDNEY

**ATRIA** BOOKS

A Division of Simon & Schuster, Inc.
1230 Avenue of the Americas
New York, NY 10020

**ATRIA** BOOKS and colophon are trademarks of Simon & Schuster, Inc.

Designed by Jaime Putorti

Manufactured in the United States of America

ISBN-13: 978-0-7432-9980-0

# YOUNG, RICH, AND DANGEROUS

## (the poem)

Young enough to make mistakes
Expose the art forms of good and bad
The choices of many and the right choices of few
Rich enough to make mistakes into catastrophe
It don't stop at dollars
I'm known by millions
Rich with knowledge and that power is dangerous
That's where your fear starts
You trying to come from your pocket instead of your heart
True youth comes from within
The only rich man is one who knows the value of life and
   death
Danger is present when consciousness is absent
Let your mind be the key to unlocking the beauty in your heart
Have Godliness in your soul
Live in it or rest in it
I'm gone

—Ruben "Big Rube" Bailey

Y'all know what this is . . .

So So Def!!!

# CONTENTS

# CONTENTS

# FOREWORD

There are three kinds of producers: the musician who plays instruments and arranges music; the beat master who's skilled with the drum machine and takes several tracks to put together a chord; and the articulator who has an idea of everything he wants to hear but expresses it verbally for others to play. Nowadays, younger producers get credit for doing a lot less on a record. Their skills are fragmented and they're lucky if they can be successful at even one of these tasks.

But not Jermaine Dupri. He possesses all of those talents and then some. Even though J.D.'s a young dude who's very much in tune with what's happening musically today, his grind is 100 percent old school. He is one of a breed, like Quincy Jones, Babyface, Jimmy Jam, and Terry Lewis, who can make a record from A to Z, from finding an artist and grooming them, to developing them vocally and making a record that's true to the character of that particular artist and yet somehow bigger. These producers don't need an established artist to make a hit. They build up the stars from scratch. The artist comes in and says, "This is what I can do." But the great producers, like J.D., take an artist's innate abilities much further—way beyond what the artist initially thought he could do.

It takes a special, visionary kind of person to pull this off. You need the greatest communication skills. You need to be able to get along with anyone anyhow. There's no room in the booth for a producer's ego. You have to manage the egos of others and yet command the artist's respect and trust at the same time. You have to have a humbleness about you as well as an aura of strength and confidence that makes people pay attention and want to give you their best. That's my man J.D. to the very core.

I first met Jermaine back in 1994 when I was performing with my act Blackstreet at the same show as him and Da Brat, who was performing her hit song "Funkdafied," a truly great record. We never really spoke at the time. We just sort of smiled and nodded at each other as we lounged around backstage. But it wasn't long before we met up again. J.D. was digging some track I wrote for Queen Pen and told me so. He's always one to give props to other producers he respects. We've been kicking it together ever since.

Pretty soon J.D. invited me and my group to perform at his birthday party in Atlanta and really laid on some first-class

Southern hospitality. After that he came to Miami to celebrate my birthday. The champagne was flowing like it does at these events, and J.D. climbed up onstage to tell the whole crowd that I was the reason he first decided to become a producer! I've never felt so honored. He puts my name out there like that all the time.

And that's the thing about J.D. He believes in educating by the example of others as well as his own. He wants kids today to understand what it takes to make it in this business and if he believes there's something to be learned from another producer's work he has no problem holding it up to the light. Many of these other producers, like Bryan Michael Cox, have been long-time protégés of Jermaine's. Today they win Grammys and enjoy accolades in their own careers as a result of what they learned in their mentor's studio, and J.D. is thrilled that he had a hand in their success.

Back in the day, no one even cared about the producing aspect of making a record. People just wanted to be artists. But these days you find a lot of people coming into our camp. They think, "I'm gonna get me a Ferrari and a Benz just like J.D." They don't know all of the grinding and process it takes to get to that level of success. They're only interested in the glamour. They don't realize it takes 150 songs with at least 50 percent of them doing well to make it to the top and stay there.

So many rappers, like Kwamé, want to become producers now that in some ways our game is even more popular than being in the spotlight as a performer. For these kids, and anyone aspiring to get into this business, this book, *Young, Rich, and Dangerous*, is truly a gift. Only someone like Jermaine, who knows it because he lives it, is in a position to deliver such necessary and relevant insights.

I'm honored to support my friend J.D. in this and any other endeavor. It's long been one of my missions in life to team up with him on a project one day. Meanwhile, I'm proud to see him take the torch and continue to run with it. Many people can get to the top, but few can maintain that position and still remember that it's the music that matters. J.D. never forgets. He's a superstar because his great music has made so many stars and touched millions of lives. But for him, it's always about the process.

—Teddy Riley, producer

# INTRODUCTION

There's a movie they made more than twenty years ago that reminds me of me—it's called *The Idolmaker*. Until a few years ago I never heard of it. It was no blockbuster. Then I was flipping through the movie channels late one night when I came across it. I was blown away by how similar the story of this hustla, played by Ray Sharkey, was to my life, or at least the essentials of it. It goes like this:

It's 1959, the era of Elvis and the pretty-boy rock stars that make young girls scream. Vinnie Vacarri, an Italian guy from New York, can sing, write songs, and move. But he ain't got the face for stardom, or at least he doesn't think he has. So instead of being the player, he decides to become the playmaker and find a guy who he can make into the star who'll sing his songs and dance his moves. Meanwhile, he'll be the dude that controls everything behind the scenes.

Vinnie keeps running into some young thug named Tommy Dee from the neighborhood who's always on him to check out his act in a local club. The kid, another Italian from the neighborhood, plays saxophone and sings a little, but Vinnie decides he ain't interested in his group when he hears the front man is some blond-haired, blue-eyed guy. "So what?" he says. He knows that's not the type who makes women crazy because he's checked out the teen magazines and the real teen idols all have slicked-back dark hair. But one night he goes to see Tommy at the club anyway.

Vinnie watches Tommy's opening moves and studies the audience's reaction. A platinum blonde with big breasts gets so excited by Tommy, who gyrates like a dirtier version of Elvis, that she looks like she's going to wet herself. But when the blue-eyed lead singer comes on, she stops bouncing and powders her nose. That's when Vinnie says to himself, "This is the guy I need for the act that's gonna make me rich. He's the one!" Not the lead singer. Tommy Dee.

Now y'all might be surprised how much some Italian dude from the Lower East Side of Manhattan has in common with a lil' African-American guy from College Park, Atlanta. But Vinnie did what I was doing for years before I saw that movie. When I discovered Kris Kross in a shopping mall, it was the girls looking and pointing at the two cute boys that caught me. Hell, those kids weren't even rapping. They were just shopping for sneakers and hanging out! They just had that lil' spark that everybody could see but only I understood.

In the movie, Vinnie takes Tommy, cleans him up, gives him words to sing and tells him how to walk, dance, talk, and dress to get past the censors, command the stage and win over the girls. He becomes like an older brother to the kid and teaches him every trick, including how to comb his hair into that puffy fifties greaser look.

Vinnie stays on Tommy, even coaching him from backstage on how to stare into the eyes of a thirteen-year-old girl in the audience. Vinnie says, "Trust me, I know all the moves and I can make this happen."

Then Tommy and Vinnie go on the road together and Vinnie pulls every string. He gets him on the radio, books him for sock hops, and makes sure his artist doesn't do something stupid like commit statutory rape with a teenybopper girl. It doesn't much matter that Tommy Dee ain't that talented or that he's borderline retarded because Vinnie not only makes the man, he puts every last bit of his energy into making sure his act's every move puts him on the path to stardom and keeps him there.

Now I'm not saying my artists are all like Tommy Dee. They all got natural talent plus star power. But the fans don't know just how much work goes on behind the scenes before they see the video or the promotional tour. The idolmaker writes the songs, produces the track, comes up with the look, deals with the knuckleheads at the label, and handles all the business. The star is the beautiful face that gets put in front of all that sweat and tears. In the movie, Vinnie does all that by himself with no one to tell him how.

But one star with a few hits ain't enough. The first time could just be dumb luck, so Vinnie has to find another kid. He's sitting in some Italian restaurant cursing out a busboy who spills something on him and suddenly realizes he's looking at the next teen idol, an even prettier, younger, and dumber dude than Tommy. This busboy never even sang a note in his life. So Vinnie takes the kid, who he decides to call Caesare, into his own home and builds him up from scratch. No one believes he can do it. Everyone doubts him, even Caesare. Tommy gets jealous and tries to sabotage the new kid's career because Vinnie's attention is all on the new guy. Vinnie tells everyone, "Please, you have to trust me, I know exactly what I'm doing." He defies the doubters and the haters and turns Caesare into an even bigger star than Tommy!

In the end, the stars all forget what Vinnie did for them and turn against him. The bloodsuckas at the big artist management companies and the record labels are quick to sign them up and steal them away. Vinnie loses it all. Once he makes his artists successful he can't control them and they forget the guy who made it all happen.

Yeah, me and Vinnie have a lot in common. I've been through all the bullshit when stars have one or two hits and suddenly get amnesia. Some are loyal and most get their memory back when they've gone out on their own and failed to make even gold records. Like my man Vinnie, I can also perform onstage, although I prefer being the playmaker, controlling everything behind the scenes. For me, being that guy who makes it all happen is more fun than being the star.

But times have changed. Lil' guys like me don't have to stay behind the curtain anymore. We're dangerous. We matter, times 10, because what we touch goes platinum and makes everybody rich. When we do our thing, all the most powerful people in the industry get on a plane and come to us to help them make hits!

There are still haters in the music industry. Jealous people are always going to come along and try to mess things up. But hip hop has given us the power. The labels know they need me if they want to stay in the game and be connected to the market, and the artists know who's going to keep their best-selling joints coming. We idolmakers can go on making hit after hit after hit until eventually we have almost as much fame, more power, and even more cold hard cash as the idols themselves.

Nowadays, the artists can't help but remember who made their careers. Hell, Mariah Carey even came up onstage with me the other day at New York's Hot 97 Summer Jam. That meant everything, because it was her way of giving me a nod to what I've done for her in front of a huge crowd of hip-hop fans. The artists, no matter how big I get, will continue to need me as long as I can keep dominating the charts.

Today, kids want to be the producers as much as they want to be the artists. Maybe more so, because they know we pull the strings. They wanna be Dr. Dre and me, because of what we do backstage, not onstage. Guys like us, and especially the ones who follow in our footsteps, aren't disposable anymore. We're young, rich, and a danger to those middle-aged executives who sit in the corner office of a record label making bad decisions because they don't understand today's music market and have nothing to do with how it gets made other than sign the checks.

The more kids come up like us, the more we're gonna take over the industry. I'm writing this book and telling my story 'cause I want to lay it out for y'all. Anyone who is hungry, ambitious, and talented can take this chance to peek backstage and inside the studio to see how it all goes down. I mean really goes down, because this life ain't nothing like what you're gonna see on un-reality shows like *American Idol*, *Rock Star*, or *Making the Band*. That shit is harmful because it makes kids think all they need is a great voice and someone else's song. Those contestants, for the most part, can only sing, but it's so much more than that. The reality of this business is way harder than anyone who hasn't been through it could know.

I still have my moments of doubt. There've been times, like last year, when it seemed like I spent a lifetime on frustrating conference calls with Virgin executives. It made me question why I'm doing all this. But when I step back, I see the impact I'm having and I know I wouldn't change a thing.

Personally, I've never been happier in the skin I'm in. I've got my girl, Janet Jackson. I'm the little guy wearing the LV sunglasses and diamond grill you see stepping on the red carpet beside her, getting interviewed by *Access Hollywood* and snapped by paparazzi for *People* magazine. I've got my Grammy, the first of what I hope will be many. I've got all the trappings. I've been buying the best rides since before I could drive and today I have nine in my driveway—Lambos, Hummers, Bentleys—you name it. I've lost count of how many pairs of sneakers I own. I've got rooms full in four different locations. I'm a ballaholic shopaholic!

I own a big mansion in Buckhead, a $5 million private studio, condos in Miami, L.A., and an apartment in the Trump Building in New York City. I own the kinds of cars and houses that some artists have to rent when they play Big Willie in their videos! Y'all must know that joint I did with Jay-Z called *Money Ain't a Thang*. That's been my lifestyle for years.

It's no secret that I enjoy those riches. I used to make a habit of flaunting my wealth. But you can't put a price on the satisfaction I get when I'm making hits and taking artists to the top. That part never gets old. The other day I got a page from Chingy, a rapper who came to me to write and produce "Pullin' Me Back," which topped the charts. He said, "J.D., I always wanted to work wit you since Kris Kross so thanks man, you don't know how much this means to me. Man, the song is number one on *Billboard* an' that's because of us. Right on, dog. Anything you need, I'm thurr." That kind of appreciation from an artist means something because it's so rare. I got all choked up.

These days I enjoy highs like that all the more because I've been through my share of lows. No one knows better than me that it takes a lot more than a bunch of stuff to feel truly successful. Fame and riches have a flip side. The music industry can be a cruel mistress. It breaks your heart over and over again.

When you strive to be the best, the disappointment of anything less than the top of the Top Ten just knocks you flat on your ass. As far as the world is concerned, you're only as good as your last hit. And most of the time it's not just one song I'm worried about, but four or five being released at the same time. Then I'm worrying all over again about what comes next.

I'll never understand these basketball stars who want to go into the music industry. They just see the red carpet stuff, the lifestyle, but that's not even 10 percent of it. They can get paid $50 million a contract, PLUS endorsement deals just to play a game that they love! But I can't just sit in my studio making music. I'm always dealing with lots of little work stuff like conference calls and meetings with label executives, trying to squeeze more cash out of a budget to get more promotion for an album that's just come out. It's tedious daytime stuff that blows up my pager and ties me up when I'd rather be making music.

Being a hitmaker ain't exactly an insurance policy for success. As long as I want to dominate the charts, I have to be on top of my game and never let myself be caught napping. In my world, there's always some new kid tappin' on your shoulder trying to break in and get past you. I always worry that too much success will make me go soft and I'll lose touch, so I'm out there all the time in the clubs, at the radio stations, making sure I stay connected with the audience.

You could argue that as far as my songwriting and producing skills are concerned, I've been on top for a while now. I'm not just frontin'. Look it up in *Billboard*, *The New York Times*, you name it. As of today, I have twenty-one multi-platinum records to my name, from Kris Kross to Usher, whose biggest hits were made by me. I've worked with Alicia Keys, Ludacris, OutKast, Jay-Z, and of course my girl, Janet.

I cowrote and produced Mariah Carey's Grammy-winning comeback album, *The Emancipation of Mimi*. One joint on that album, "We Belong Together," had more spins on radio than any other song in the history of music. Just a few weeks later my artists Dem Franchize Boyz hit the top of the charts.

I'm that lil' guy working the soundboard, making the biggest stars in hip hop, R&B, and pop. I've been in the business for a decade and a half and have tens of millions in record sales. I've made more hit songs than any other producer since the start of this millennium. I own my own label, So So Def, and I know my way around the executive floor of major record labels.

That's why I'm calling this book "Young, Rich, and Dangerous." At 34, I'm still young, especially when you compare me to most other senior music executives. I'm rich, with full-blown baller status. And I'm dangerous. My hands-on grind with the music and my closeness to what's going on in the streets and the clubs makes me a threat to all of the competition out there.

No one else on the business side of music has my sense of what's happening on the front lines of the music scene. People running record labels today don't have the ears to pick out what's hot in all the small clubs and strip joints across the country where it's all happening. But I'm out there on the streets like no one else.

If that sounds cocky, you wouldn't be the first person to think it. People don't like my swagger. But they don't understand it's taken me a minute to believe in myself all the way. The industry was quick to dismiss dudes like me from the South, so I needed my cockiness to carry me through.

My achievements didn't come easy, no matter how it might look to people looking in from the outside. When people see me, they just assume I'm some guy who never had to struggle. To them I'm just some little kid who got lucky with my first act, Kris Kross. They didn't see me during those two years I spent working on a four-track in a little room in my mom's house, making that first album. They just know it sold eight million.

For all y'all who want to know what life is like behind the boards, I'm gonna take you right there. By the end of this book—which I think of as an album featuring all the tracks of my life—you're gonna understand the mysteries of the studio, the process of working with the artist, the business of dealing with corporate suits, the stress of releasing an album at the right time, and the right way to get the most spins on radio and blow up the sales. You're gonna understand that it can be the most frustrating, tedious, crazy, exhausting, exhilarating, beautiful, and rewarding life for anyone who can stand the heat. You'll also come to realize that out of every 100 kids I put in my shoes, 98 of them won't make it.

I'm not offering readers a blueprint. It'd be pretty hard for anyone to follow me in my life. My path wasn't exactly a mistake-free, straight line to success. I recently won some Urban

League "Influencer" award. It's supposed to mean that my example is inspiring the next generation of young black people to succeed. But I'm not so sure I deserved it. I'm not pretending I'm out to change anyone's life. I'm just telling it like it is. If it prepares some kid who's thinking about being in this business by opening his eyes to what's real, so be it. The best way to teach something is to tell a story, and the story I know best is my own.

Will I get personal? Nothing's more personal to me than this business. I spent the better part of last year, and part of the year before, executive producing my girl Janet's album. That was serious business close to my heart. The music industry is the air that I breathe and the blood that pumps through my veins. When I work with an artist, I become them and a piece of me lives on in each of their songs. They're like family. In the early days, some of them got so cozy they even lived in my house! Now I'm inviting you to open the door, turn the page, and step inside.

# THE LIFE OF J.D.

1972: Jermaine Dupri is born in Asheville, North Carolina; family moves to College Park, Atlanta

1975: As three-year-old, plays drums and stuns Aunt Lucy with perfect rhythm and pitch

1982: Steals show with dance moves at Diana Ross concert

1983: Father moves out; Grandpa Dee passes; moves to house on Judy Lane with mother Tina

1984: Joins New York Fresh Fest as opening act, tours with them over next three years

1985: Meets Chad Elliot on tour; spends summer with him in Brooklyn discovering the New York hip-hop scene; father Michael attempts to put out a Chad and J.D. duo rap record;

becomes fast friends with neighborhood kids Eddie Weathers and Daryl Barr

1986: Launches thriving mixtape enterprise, So So Def

1987: Discovers and develops girl group Silk Tymes Leather

1989: Establishes So So Def Productions; releases Silk Tymes' *Ain't Where Ya From . . . It's Where Ya At* on Geffen

1990–1991: Spots two kids shopping in Greenbriar Mall and turns them into Kris Kross, spends next year working on album; releases Javier & the Str8Jackers on Ichiban; does demo for TLC

1992: Releases first Kris Kross album, *Totally Krossed Out* and quickly sells over four million copies; single "Jump" breaks records; inks $10 million deal with Columbia, forms joint venture label So So Def Records

1993–1994: Discovers, signs, and develops multiplatinum So So Def artists Xscape and Da Brat

1995–1996: Teams up with Mariah Carey for the first time on "Always Be My Baby"; outside production and remix projects take off; produces Bass All-Stars records with employee and future King of Crunk, Lil Jon

1997: Named EMI Songwriter of the Year; wins Hot 97 Remixer of the Year; starts working with Usher on sophomore album *My Way* and puts him on path to stardom

1998: May 15, daughter Shaniah is born; releases first solo album, *Life in 1472*; gets nominated for Grammy for best rap album; releases debut Jagged Edge album *A Jagged Era*

1999–2000: Wins five ASCAP awards, meets and produces Lil' Bow Wow, produces and remixes for stream of top artists from Elton John to TLC, Monica, Usher, Run-DMC, Kelly Price, etc.; produces Bow Wow's *Beware of Dog*, breaking more records in rap

2001: Produces remix for Janet Jackson's "Someone to Call My Lover," the beginning of a beautiful friendship; produces "What's Going On" for Artists United Against AIDS with Bono; nominated for producer/songwriter Grammy for Alicia Keys's "Girlfriend" on *Songs in A Minor*, builds SouthSide studio with money from Sony

2002: Becomes president of Atlanta chapter of the National Academy of Recording Arts and Sciences; beefs with Dr. Dre; leaves Sony/Columbia, gets a visit from the IRS

2003–2004: Joins Arista as president of urban music and cuts another label deal, signs Anthony Hamilton, Bone Crusher, J-Kwon to So So Def; produces Usher's multiplatinum album *Confessions*; steps down from Academy after Super Bowl

2005: Joins Virgin Records; signs Dem Franchize Boyz; produces history-making Mariah Carey hit "We Belong Together"

2006–2007: Wins first Grammy for best R&B song "We Belong Together"; starts production on Janet's *20 Y.O.*; becomes youngest individual to be inducted into the Georgia Music Hall of Fame; leaves Virgin; to be continued . . .

# YOUNG, RICH,
## AND DANGEROUS

# 1

## FRESH AZIMIZ

Back in the old days, 15 years ago, Atlanta's music scene wasn't in Atlanta at all. It was about an hour's drive north of the city in a suburb called Alpharetta.

A mostly white, affluent neighborhood in Fulton County, Georgia, ain't exactly what you'd expect of a mecca for all urban artists, producers, and musicians coming up in the South. But it was there, deep inside the Alpharetta Country Club, on an estate surrounded by golf courses and lawn ornaments, where Antonio "L.A." Reid bought his McMansion and set up studios for LaFace Records, the label he started with Arista and his partner, Kenneth "Babyface" Edmonds.

That crib was crazy. Besides the house where L.A. lived with his then wife Pebbles and their kids, the compound had another huge building housing everything a music guy could want: recording and mixing studios, a dance rehearsal room, a hair salon, and a kitchen with a full-time professional chef to fix a lil' snack for the artists and studio engineers between sessions. L.A. designed the whole thing to be a place where he could develop artists from scratch. Their moves, their image, their voice training all went down inside those walls.

On any given day or night the driveway would be deep with Benzes, Bentleys, Beemers, Rolls-Royces, and Porsches. TLC, Goodie Mob, Anita Baker, Whitney Houston, and Bobby Brown were just a few of the artists who passed through those doors. One day I was there waiting to mix a record and Toni Braxton was laying down vocals with L.A. in the next studio, Dallas Austin was in the kitchen waiting on some lunch, Babyface was at the piano composing a song, and Chilli and T-Boz from TLC were downstairs getting their hair fixed by Pebbles.

Back then, I never had any direct dealings with L.A. or Babyface myself. But like anyone in the ATL, I was well aware of who they were. Those two brought some real star power to a scene that was always being overlooked by the music industry in favor of New York or the West Coast. The fact that they were on our doorstep was creating some buzz.

They were the idolmakers of their day. Babyface was the guy who wrote hit songs for Whitney Houston, Aretha Franklin, Gladys Knight, and just about every other great female singer at the time. L.A. was the guy who signed all the talent.

Most kids hoping to make it in the industry beat a path

straight to L.A.'s door. When I made TLC's demo tape they took it first to Pebbles. Anyone with aspirations and a shred of talent made the trek to Alpharetta. Usher auditioned there when he was 13. He walked in, introduced himself as LaFace's "next big star" and told L.A. he was gonna own that house some day. A few years and a couple of Grammys later, he did.

But I wasn't one of those kids. As far as I was concerned, I already had my shine on. It was 1992 and I was fresh off my success with Kris Kross. I was 19 and I'd just seen my first big check for $1 million. My act's single, "Jump" was dominating the charts. It stayed number one on the *Billboard* 100 for eight whole weeks. No one had seen a kiddie sensation like that in rap music before.

There hadn't been a faster selling single in 15 years. My two stars, Chris Kelly and Chris Smith, were all over the TV, appearing on *The Oprah Winfrey Show*, *In Living Color*, *The Tonight Show*, and dominating the videoplay on MTV and BET. In all, we sold eight million copies of that first album, *Totally Krossed Out*. As far as I was concerned, my career was already on fire.

Me and my best friend Eddie Weathers had a lot of celebrating to do. We were popping tags all over the place. After years making do with the sales rack at JCPenney we were flying up to New York and Chicago for spending sprees, buying ourselves diamond chains and gold watches. I was heading straight into my young, fly, and flashy days.

I bought my mom a shiny, new blue BMW convertible and the salesman talked me into buying another Beemer for myself.

Meanwhile, I was shopping around for a nice big ranch house so we could move out of our tiny place in College Park.

I only went to L.A.'s place in Alpharetta because I needed to use his fancy hi-tech mixing equipment to finish up some production work for TLC. I was still working from my little bedroom on Judy Lane and relying on some cheap Radio Shack equipment. There weren't too many state-of-the-art studios around Atlanta at the time.

I never even spoke to L.A. or Babyface except to say "hey." They couldn't have been more than 30, but to me they seemed old, like those Motown dudes who were more into soul and R&B. They'd both been in bands in the eighties, and their music credentials were real, but with L.A. especially I felt the generation gap. He always seemed like he is now: slick, polished, and corporate. I didn't think they were up on what was happening in the hip-hop movement. I respected them, but I reckoned they didn't have a whole lotta relevance to a young buck like me.

Then one day they threw a party. After a couple of drinks I clocked L.A. and Babyface sitting by themselves. They were on the patio off the recording room, where the studio engineers went out for smoke breaks. I decided to sit down and join them. My newfound success made me feel bold enough to take my place at their table, and I was curious to get to know the other players in Atlanta's budding music scene.

We talked for a bit about the business. L.A. threw me a few polite questions about how it was going with Kris Kross. I was proud of the fact that my act was still killing the charts and I guess I let them know, figuring they'd share in my excitement. I didn't mean to sound boastful, but I guess they saw me as a cocky lil' dude.

That whole time Babyface didn't say a word, but there must've been something about my swagger that bugged him. When he finally opened his mouth he cut me to the bone:

"Good for you that you've got your little song," he said. "But one hit doesn't count for much. You gotta have three or four hits before you can really call yourself a success."

That hurt my feelings. I didn't know what to say, so I slumped in my chair for a second. I thought to myself, "Hell, I haven't seen either of y'all coming out with no number one hits lately."

Plenty of people assumed I was just some nobody who got lucky, but my success with Kris Kross was no overnight fluke. I'd been working toward it for years, making mixtapes since I was 12; producing another group, Silk Tymes Leather, when I was 14; and struggling for almost two years to get attention from a record label that would help me break Chris and Chris. A lil' nod instead of a slap from my elders would have been nice.

Then I thought about it some more, "Maybe Babyface has a point. I gotta keep pushing myself if I want to truly be somebody in this business. I can't stop now."

I had two choices. I could have said, "To hell with it. I'm still just a kid and I'm gonna have fun on this ride while it lasts." I could have enjoyed my moment for what it was. I could have spent all the money from my check until it was gone, which I was already halfway to doing, and been content to live out my days as a one-hit wonder. Or I could decide that the life I really wanted would be all about me getting my grind on and slaving for the next hit, and the hit after that, and the hit after that. I guess it really wasn't a choice. I couldn't stop because I'd always want more.

Babyface's tough words were the best things that anyone could have said to me back then. They stuck with me so hard that I even programmed that philosophy into my pager. To this day, anyone who ever gets a message from me sees this tagline:

"When you win one time they call you a champion, when you win four times they call you a dynasty, when you win 21 times they call you So So Def!"

Yeah, that's right. Today I have more than 20 top hits and they keep coming. I should put one of those signs up like they have at McDonald's that says, "Over one billion served."

Because of guys like me, the music scene moved south on the Interstate to take over the heart of the ATL. To let people know we're here, I pay $8,000 a month for a big Day-Glo yellow sign by the I-85 that says, ATLANTA, HOME OF SO SO DEF RECORD-INGS. I was inspired by Berry Gordy's Motown billboard in Detroit that says, WELCOME TO MOTOR CITY, HOME OF HITSVILLE U.S.A. But maybe I should add a digital counter to keep track of all of those charts I'm slaying!

Not that I intend to rest on past success. I have to keep it turned on to keep turning out the hits. I wrote this poem three years ago to remind myself what it takes to win:

One that neva sleeps,
One that keeps his ear on the streets,
One that sets trends without tryin'
And all the time, no matter what, they shinin'.
One that looks and listens closer
Than other niggas.
Big, but constantly thinking of ways to get bigger.
One that's looked at to come thru in the clutch,
Highly talked about, but don't give a fuck.
Whether he plays ball, works in Corporate America,
Sings or produces,
If this person was to shut down shop
All hell would break loose!
Motivated by younger people,
That wanna be in his shoes,
Knowing how to do nothin' else but win,
But ain't scared to lose,
Cause a loss every once in a while,
Is what makes you turn it on,
And do what you do, but be twice as strong,
The best is a person that's out
To do shit that ain't neva been done,
This is my definition.
Don't know about you,
But I'm one.

I put those words on a plaque and stuck it on the wall of my studio for everyone to see. I'm not saying I'm the best, but I strive to be. There are plenty of producers, like Quincy Jones, who've had more hits than me. That's why I keep running. I'm a beast in the game who won't quit until everyone else is beat.

# 2

# WELCOME TO ATLANTA

Growing up, I was a poster child for latchkey kids. My dad wasn't around much—he was always off working as a roadie for concert tours, or having too much fun with the women and partying. I spent days at a time without seeing my mom, who was working as many as three jobs by the time I was 10.

People don't leave their kids on their own nowadays. But back then, it was no big deal to leave a kid by himself in the house. You did what you had to do. I never thought of all that independence and solitude while I was coming up as a bad thing. I made good use of my freedom. Being home alone gives a kid's imagination plenty of space to roam. My parents were too young to know better anyway. My mother got pregnant when she was just 17 and my father was all of 18.

My mom was born Cecilia Mosley. A pretty lil' southern

belle from Asheville, North Carolina, she came up living a sheltered but comfortable life under her parents' roof. My grandmother was a strict, churchgoing Baptist lady who kept a close eye on my mother.

As a teenager, my mother had dreams of being a dancer like Lola Falana. She reckons she could have out-danced her idol if she hadn't had me. But her dancing career was over before it got started. When she was getting ready to go to college to study dancing, Granny made her go into the nursing program instead. Something about music and dancing always made my grandmother a tad suspicious. Maybe she was nervous it would lead to loose behavior. She even made my Grandpa Dee choose between her and his saxophone! He picked her, but that didn't stop him from playing his sax on the sly.

In the end, my mom never made it to college. She used to hang out all the time with her best friend, Johnnie Mae Nelson, the daughter of Granny's best friend. The two girls did everything together. It was all innocent fun until Johnnie Mae's cousin, my father Michael Mauldin, came calling from a nearby town. My mother didn't stand a chance.

My father was, and still is, a tall, smooth-talkin' dude who knew how to charm the ladies and usually got his way. He came from a well-to-do Catholic family in North Carolina but he had big-city ambitions to make it in the music industry.

After all, it was 1972, the year of Motown's heyday, when Berry Gordy was the richest black man in America. Michael Jackson's "Ben," The Jackson 5's "Little Bitty Pretty One," and the Temptations' "Papa Was a Rollin' Stone," were always playing on the radio. There was magic being made up there in Detroit and my dad was one of many other young, hip black men with musical ambitions who wanted to be a part of that life.

He was just starting out as a roadie and a drummer who got the occasional professional gig, but he was convinced that he was going to make it big as a manager or producer and he blew a lot of smoke about what he was gonna do when he made it.

My mom must've been impressed because nine months later I was born. My father decided to call me Jermaine, after Jermaine Jackson, thinking it would go well with his own name, Michael, and bring to mind some association with the Jackson Five. Hah! Who'd have guessed that twenty-seven years later I'd be dating their baby sister!

Names mattered to my dad, and whatever he picked for his firstborn son had to reflect well on his own ambitions. He picked Dupri for my middle name, after Cornell Dupree, a funk guitar player from New Orleans. My dad liked the exotic French sound of that name, but mostly it was because he couldn't stop playing "The Ghetto," a song on Donny Hathaway's LP where Dupree was playing lead guitar. Thanks to Michael Mauldin, I was one of those rare kids who was actually born with a stage name. By my father's design, I had two musical namesakes. Music was my destiny.

My mom went along with the names, like she did with most things in those early days. My dad was in charge. They got married and, before I could crawl, my dad moved us to Atlanta, the nearest big city where he figured he could find more production gigs.

We moved to a small apartment in a housing estate called Dhorage right by the airport. I still pass by the estate in my car and shake my head at how run-down and sad the place looks. It didn't look much better 30 years ago.

Even though we were poor, we were a happy family for a minute. My mom was still in love with my dad and there were some good times despite all our money problems. Sometimes she struggled with the fact that her husband was a control freak. Dad always insisted on deciding what jobs my mother did, what she wore, where she went. Once, when she changed her hairstyle after a trip back home to Asheville, my father made it known he didn't like it by dragging her into the shower to wet it down and make it disappear. As far as he was concerned, image was everything.

But it was easy enough to forgive and forget whenever my dad went over the line. He had the charm and smiles to help us get past it. Whenever he got some extra cash, which wasn't often, he bought us all presents and nice clothes, and treated himself too. He snuck us in to see the concerts he was working as production manager. When he was home, it was like one big party and all his musician friends would come over to kick it with him. That was real excitement for a three-year-old.

Even as a toddler, my dad was always pushing me in my musical ambitions. At three, he bought me my first drum set. I could bang out a beat perfectly before I could speak.

I'm too young to remember, but I'm told my dad used to take me along to studio sessions for Brick, a local funk band he worked with. Pretty soon I was playing the drum tracks of the entire Brick catalogue.

One of my earliest memories is of me wandering into a room where a couple of my dad's drummer friends were playing along to a tune on the stereo on a full-size set of drums. I must've been about five, but I walked right up to them and stood in between to get an eye-level view of what was going on. I stood there all quiet and watched. There's a picture of me standing between those two guys, with just my eyes peeking over the cymbals, but I didn't even know it was being taken at the time.

I could recite songs word for word by the time I turned seven. One time, we went over to my father's sister, Aunt Lucy's house. She was a schoolteacher and knew all about aptitude tests, so she decided to show off and test my learning skills by tapping beats out on a table. No matter how complicated the beats got, she couldn't trip me up. I tapped them back at her in rapid fire. Then the oldest of old-school rap started playing on the radio: "Rapper's Delight" by the Sugar Hill Gang.

After the song played I grabbed a hairbrush and, pretending it was a mic, stood up on a little red rocking chair, and rapped out the whole song perfectly, line by line, making the beat by rocking that little chair back and forth.

Aunt Lucy was trippin' so much, she just about fell over. She declared me "gifted." Not that my family could afford any special schooling for me. Money was almost always scarce. My dad's income was on-again, off-again and he made it next to impossible for my mom to work. One time, when she had a job as a waitress, he showed up at the restaurant late at night with a few of his friends, drunk. She had to quit after that.

Like most of our neighbors, there was a period when we lived on food stamps. There were weeks when we got down to our last box of Rice-A-Roni or Kraft dinners. I was born liking fly clothes and shoes, but I made do with stuff on discount at Kmart. I knew enough not to bug my mother for the fancy labels. I could see she was struggling. People just assume that I always had money because I was so young when I first made it, but I had to walk up the ladder too.

Mom and Dad hid it well from me, but things started unraveling inside their marriage early on. It was getting so shaky, that I got sent back to Asheville a few times to live with my grandparents on my mother's side. Matter of fact, I was tossed around quite a bit in those days. I only found out recently that the two sets of grandparents were fighting over me.

My grandma on my dad's side didn't think my mother was old enough to take care of me, so I had to stay with my Grandma Mauldin for a while. But my grandparents on my mother's side, especially Grandpa Dee, wouldn't have that. Pretty soon, they sent for me to live in Asheville, where I started going to school and summer camp.

I was happy. Those months in Asheville were some of my best childhood memories. Grandpa Dee was the numbers man in town and a real old-school hustla. He was a character, always out in the street doin' his thing.

Grandpa worked nine-to-five during the week as a glazier, installing windows in all the big office buildings around town. But every weekend he was on the block, working Eagle Street, the main drag where all the black nightclubs and restaurants were located back in the day. I tagged along as his lil' sidekick and watched him as he went around the neighborhood taking the numbers for that week's bet. I spent so much time with him he became like a surrogate dad to me.

The numbers racket wasn't exactly legal. Instead of horses or sports, poor black folks would play a number each week at a dollar or so a bet. My gramps was the guy who collected the cash and put up the numbers, passing along the winnings if anyone guessed right. The more people he could get in on the game the bigger the pot and the more money he could keep for himself.

Back in the day, it was the Italian Mafia who ran the numbers, but it got to the point where it was all black folks betting, so we took it over from the mob. The game worked like a pyramid, with the most powerful runner being in charge of a region and collecting the biggest percentage of winnings. Grandpa was high up in the chain, because he pretty much ran Asheville. He was so slick with it that he had connections with all the right people, and someone in the police department would tip him off when they were gonna raid. I'd go with him when he stashed the numbers, names, and cash in one of his little hidey-holes around town.

That lil' underworld life fired up my childhood imagination. I think that's how I got so into those *Godfather* movies and *Scarface*. Stories about *la famiglia* were dope to me. The honor code of the mob, and how they'd whack the bad guys who broke it, I loved it! One of the only times I ever got nervous meeting a celebrity apart from Janet (and that was for different reasons), was when I saw Al Pacino at the Four Seasons in L.A. I went up to him and said, "Hey, Tony, how ya doin'?" He winced a little before he smiled, but I couldn't help myself. No one played a mobster better than him.

Grandpa Dee wasn't quite that shady. He was the cool dude in town with the gold teeth and the fast wit, always fun to watch do his thing. All the local hoochie mammas loved him. I must've got my business sense and hustle from those days running around town with him. Maybe that's also where I caught my gambling bug.

But mostly he just took care of me. He used to cook the best soul food I ever tasted. He made me chitlins with gravy and pork-knuckle stew. When the weather turned cool up there in the Appalachian Mountains, he'd build a fire in the big 'ole fireplace they had in the middle of the house.

Back home in Atlanta, I was living pretty much a normal little kid's life. Church on Sundays was a regular thing. My mother converted to Catholicism at my dad's insistence and I was the only black altar boy at our church.

But it was usually just me and my mother. Even though my parents kept their problems to themselves, I started noticing that my dad was spending a lot less time around the house. Like most other musicians, he was drawn to the nightlife. According to my mother he had a weakness for women and all the other temptations that go along with being in that world of roadies and performers. A little hustlin' revenue would tide him over between production gigs. My mom said she didn't want him bringing any of that life back to the house. For days at a time, I wouldn't see him.

My father was just being human. He was still young. It's easy to slip up when you're struggling in this industry. I see it all the time. Even today, most kids think you get into this business by selling dope first. In neighborhoods like ours, I could have easily gone that way myself. There were always opportunities and times when I could have really used the cash. But I was determined to stay away from it. That game was a distraction from music and dancing. I didn't need the $300 sneakers that badly. Besides, my mother was working hard just so I wouldn't have to go into that life.

I was no angel. I had plenty of opportunities to act up and get into mischief. My mother was putting herself through nursing school and picking up work where she could. I didn't see my dad much except for when there was some show in town. He was on the road a lot and had a few women on the side, so he'd usually crash nights and weekends somewhere else. I had plenty of dogs and a cat for company, but my furry lil' friends weren't about to stop me from indulging in my destructive side.

There were a couple of occasions when I nearly burned the

house down. I was the kid who liked setting ants on fire with a magnifying glass. One time I got bored and decided to entertain myself by playing with firecrackers. I set them up on the citronella mosquito torches we had lining the front porch. They blew up and citronella gunk slimed the entire front of the house.

I had a lot of toys back then. Still do. I'm a collector and I keep hundreds of action figures along the ledges of my recording studio. But I'm not overly attached to them. One day when I was about 10 I decided to send my Michael Jackson doll on a little trip. I attached his head to Hulk Hogan's body to keep it stable and fired a Fourth of July rocket at his head. My mom wasn't real happy when she came home to find burn marks along half the side of our house!

It's just as well there were other distractions for a restless lil' dude like me. In the early eighties, things were getting slow on the music scene. To get by, one of my father's jobs was running a video arcade in the new Atlanta airport. He'd bring me out there with him sometimes. Some of Grandpa Dee was already starting to rub off on me, 'cause I spent those days hustlin' passengers for the baggage carts they couldn't bring through security. I returned them and kept the quarters to spend on candy and sodas. To this day, when I pass through the airport, some of those shoe-shine guys still remember me as the kid with the baggage carts.

I didn't need the change to play all those games. My dad had keys to all the machines. I spent hours in that place playing

Centipede, Super Mario Brothers, Battlestar Galactica. It was paradise. I'm still addicted to gaming. I can spend all night on my PlayStation 2. It drives some of the artists crazy.

Those first arcade games must've helped my hand-eye coordination, because years later my dad pointed something out to me.

"Jermaine, you move your hands and work your drum machine like it's a video game," he said. "You makin' beats like you tryin' to kill that centipede!"

I hardly think about it when I'm in that zone, but it could have something to do with why my hands work so fast.

All in all, my come up was regular. For the most part, my childhood was fun and I did all the normal stuff kids do. I've never tried to pretend I was living some hard ghetto life. We started out as poor and worked our way up to borderline middle class. I went to grade school and junior high. I played in the Pop Warner League from the time I was five. I played just about every position on the team: running back, fullback, wide receiver. I wasn't big but I was strong and I could run fast. For a second I even wanted to be a professional player. It was my drive to win that was talking.

But music soon took possession of my soul. After drums, I wanted to play guitar. Then it was the piano. My folks got me lessons and I lasted about three months. I hated having any kind of formal training. I didn't want to waste time learning scales, theory, and this that and a third. I wanted my teacher to teach me how to play the songs I already had buzzing around in my head. They told me to be patient and I said, "Nah, to hell with that, I want to play what I hear!"

Sometimes I regret not having a formal music education. Quincy Jones, my greatest mentor, can read, write, and play his own music. Now that I'm grown, I can see the advantages. Early on, it would have saved me hours of studio time if I could translate the songs into notes written on a piece of paper. These days I have sound engineers who are classically trained in music, and one of my producers, Manuel Seal, is a genius on keyboards. I just have to hum a few bars and he gets it. But in the beginning, it could take me all night to get the sound exactly the way I heard it in my head. Then again, not knowing what I was doing was how I came up with a sound that was my own.

My clash with the piano teacher summed up how I felt about school in general. I always wanted to get from A to B as fast as possible and keep it moving. I never felt other people's ways were fast enough for me. I couldn't stand sitting in a classroom and being told. I wanted to get out there and find out for myself.

I had so much energy in my early years, I was probably more into dancing than learning instruments. I had moves I practiced all the time. You know how certain little kids dance around in front of the mirror at home? That was me. I used to try out my moves and think, "I'm tha shit!"

I got a chance to prove it when I was nine and my mom took me to see a Diana Ross concert. My dad was working on the production crew that night and he got us seats near the front. I'd been around musicians before, but a real Motown diva was a big deal. I got all dressed up with my Jheri-curled hair, lil' tweed jacket, and my prized pair of Jordache jeans.

We had great seats, right up on the ninth row. About half-way through the show, my mom had to go to the bathroom, so she asked a security guard to keep an eye on me and told me, "DON'T MOVE!"

Just after she left, Ms. Ross called all the kids from the front rows to join her up onstage and dance. She sang, "I'm Coming Out," and about 20 of them got up there and started moving, but not real well. Meanwhile I was grooving in my seat, and all the audience members around me started shouting and eggin' me on, "Go on up there, go on!"

I didn't want my mother to be mad so I stayed put. Mean-while my dad was trying to get to me from the middle of the arena, where he was working up by the sound board. He didn't want me to miss my spot in the limelight. The security guard, a woman, took pity on me so she said, "It's okay little boy, I got your back, you go on up there and dance."

All the other kids had just left by the time I ran up on the stage, and Miss Ross was talking to some guys in the band, so she didn't notice me at first. Then she turned around and said, "Oh, hello, who's this coming up here? You wanna dance?"

"Yeah," I said.

"Okay, then let me see what you can do."

The band started playing "Upside Down," her big disco hit from that year, and I did my thing. At the time, the Michael

Jackson craze was just getting started, and kids everywhere were trying to do the moonwalk, but I had all those moves down. I was popping, spinning, and getting down and the audience erupted. All I could hear was, "*Haaaaaaaaaaaaa!*"

I felt comfortable up there dancing, like it was my rightful place. I didn't freeze or think for a second about the thousands of people hollering at me. I was just in my own head enjoying what I was doing. After a while, Miss Ross started worrying that things had gone too far and she was letting herself be upstaged, so she said, "Whoa, that's enough now. Hold it!"

The band stopped playing, I stopped moving, and then she asked me my name.

"Jermaine? I know someone named Jermaine," she joked. Of course, she was referring to my namesake Jermaine Jackson, another member of the Motown family. They were all pretty tight back then. Then she asked, "Do you do anything else besides dance?"

"Nah," I said. My self-promotion skills weren't exactly up to speed back then. Then I was dismissed with an "Okay, go on back to your seat little boy." I wasn't invited backstage or anything.

As me and my mother were leaving the stadium, crowds started mobbing us. "That's the little kid who was up on the stage by himself!" someone yelled as we squeezed out of the building. The next day, the story of the little kid who stole the show was written up in the newspaper—my first piece of press coverage!

Yeah, I liked the attention. I guess I wanted more, because it wasn't long after that I started going around the neighborhoods of College Park doing dance contests. I perfected all my Michael Jackson moves. I had all the gear: the loafers, glitter socks, and pants that stopped at the ankle. Sometimes I even brought out the one glove. But I took it a step further and taught myself how to really break-dance. I could throw myself on the ground, spin on my head, walk up the side of a wall, flip, bend, and bounce like I was made of rubber.

I won each time. I was young, and small for my age, so people thought it was cute. I used that to my advantage.

A little redheaded white kid from the neighborhood named Danny was my sidekick. Atlanta was pretty segregated back then, but people must've liked seeing our mixed race duo—the little black kid and the white kid—both dancing together all ghetto like that. My mom would drive us around to all the talent shows at the schools, churches, and community centers and we always won the battle. I lost track of Danny years ago, but back then we were a team.

Around the same time, my father started getting more work as a production guy. He wasn't home much, but his gear was there. Even when me and my mom moved into a small house on Judy Lane in College Park a few years later, and long after my parents had split, my dad made his presence felt by storing staging platforms and lighting equipment in the garage. It was just more stuff to fuel my dreams about being in that world.

Meanwhile, my dad was getting ambitious for me. He used his inside track at the shows he was working to get me up on-stage. When Herbie Hancock passed through town, me and Danny were the opening act and backup dancers for his hit song "Rockit." We even got to go to New Orleans with the tour. I was starting to get a reputation on the local music and concert scene as the pop-lockin' kid with the Jheri curl.

But that first taste of what was to come was followed by one of the saddest days of my life. I was 11 when Grandpa Dee, my first real hero, passed. He was only in his early fifties, but he had high blood pressure, diabetes, high cholesterol—all the health issues that plague black men even when they're seem-ingly way too young to have such problems. My whole world went dark.

I can still remember sitting there in the church with my mother and staring at the open casket at the funeral in Ashe-ville. There were hundreds of people there. Seemed like half the town was paying respect.

At one point I could have sworn I saw Grandpa Dee walk right past me. It would have been just like him to pull that one last great hustle. It really spooked me. But it was only my Uncle Hubert. I'd never seen any of them before, but Grandpa Dee had three brothers who looked almost exactly like him. Now that I'm grown, everyone says I look exactly like my grandfa-ther—same face, same short, stocky build.

For months afterward, I was so sad it hurt. I actually felt physical pain, like a headache in my whole body. Years later, whenever I'd stare into the fire, I could swear I saw Grandpa Dee's face.

I think I took his death so hard because I somehow knew he'd be missing out on all the success I have today. I wanted him around to see some of it. That known hurt through my body was my DNA telling me so. I don't believe anything that's happened in my life is a coincidence. The plan for me to make music was in play before I was born. My life as J.D., "uber producer" and "music mogul" was preordained. Grandpa Dee, frustrated musician and savvy street hustla, was the older blueprint version of me. More than anyone, it was my grandfather who would have appreciated how far I've come.

# 3

# FREAKS COME OUT AT NIGHT

Normal childhood was over for me before I was even 12 years old. The trips to Asheville were much less of a regular thing. Grandpa Dee's death also had an effect on my mother. It forced her to grow up into the fearsome woman she is now. For years she wouldn't say shit. She'd just lean back and let my father run the show. Then it was like somebody flipped a switch. No one dares mess with Miss Tina now!

She took charge of the family and finally broke it off with my dad. My mom supported the two of us with three jobs as a home-care nurse, making extra money looking after a sick old man during the night shift. I was home alone more than ever. But I was cool with that. I had my dogs, my toys, and my music. A big opportunity was also coming my way. Pretty soon, I'd hardly be home at all.

By 1983, my dad was starting to get more work as a road manager and head of production crew for the different acts that were coming up. After working for S.O.S. Band, he found himself a gig as one of the production managers for the New York City Fresh Festival, the first big national tour for rappers. Run-DMC, Grandmaster Flash, the Fat Boys, Whodini, Kurtis Blow, you name it, they were all on the bill. It was the who's who of the rap world just as hip hop was coming into its heyday.

Even though he'd more or less moved out, me and my dad still had a relationship, but it mostly revolved around the music business. At times we were more like manager/artist than father/son. He knew full well I'd want in on the Fresh Fest and he had his own plans for my career, so when the tour passed through Atlanta he got me a cameo dancing in the opening act.

Unlike hip-hop tours nowadays, the Fresh Fest budget was tiny. As long as I was entertaining the crowds, they weren't about to turn down free child labor. When I started performing, the audience loved it and that was that. I secured myself a spot as the opening act. That was fine with me!

There was just one problem: my mom. She wasn't about to have her child go off on tour with a bunch of rappers without any supervision. The government was also gonna have a problem with me skipping school and not having a tutor on the road. There were hardly any kid acts in the rap music game back then, and my mom worried about how some of the guys on the tour might influence me. In the end, I don't know what finally convinced her to let me go. Maybe she wanted me to spend time with a dad I hardly ever saw. Most likely, she just didn't want to deny her son the dream she once had to be a dancer.

My dad knew he'd be too busy with running the production, getting the acts on and off the stage, and getting the lighting and sound right, to keep a close eye on me. He used his powers of persuasion to convince his sister Lucy, who was just coming out of a divorce, to come join us on the road and be my teacher and legal guardian. But getting me to sit still and study with idols like Run-DMC floating around wasn't going to be easy.

That tour changed my life. The schedule was crazy. We did 50 cities in three months. We went on the road and performed four or five nights a week for weeks at a time. We'd pull up into a town, hit the hotel, rehearse or do some radio, grab some food, do the show, hit a party, and start all over again the next day and the day after that. It got to be habit-forming. I don't think I've slowed down since.

Once I got a taste of that life I was hooked. Everyone treated me like a lil' grown-up. I rolled deep. I had my own valet to help me with costume changes and hustle me on and off the stage. I ran wild, playing jokes on the roadies, and mixing it up with all the different acts. Back in those days, hip hop was getting big, but it wasn't as huge as it is now and the rappers' egos were more or less in check. It was the tour that made all other rap tours like "Def Jam's Survival of the Illest" in '98 even possible, because it was the first to prove live hip-hop music could make money.

People from acts like Whodini and the Fat Boys were accessible back then. They let me hang out with them and, backstage and onstage, I studied their every move. I learned how they rhymed and I studied how they scratched. Aunt Lucy could never find me to do my homeschooling lessons because I was always too busy working on my favorite subject.

To me the guys on the tour were kinda like the cool older kids in school. They tolerated their underage mascot. Sometimes I got in their way; usually on purpose. Just to get a reaction I'd "interrupt" when they were trying to pick up girls. I was like Bow Wow when he first came to me as an 11-year-old rapper: just a regular rotten kid who'd run around, hide, and drive everyone nuts until it was time to get to work.

I'd duck Lucy and hide around the sound and stage equipment. I had a big problem with sitting still. Even today, the idea that I'm doing something because I *have* to makes me go and do just the opposite. I'll put it off and play a video game. I get more done when I'm mixing up work time and play time and I don't have to think, "Oh, this is me working now." Corporate stuff aside, it's all part of the same process.

By the second year of the tour, I had a partner in crime who was just as good at escaping from schoolwork. Chad Elliott, the only other guy my age on the tour, used to rap and dance with the Fat Boys. Chad was a child actor from New York who got his start in Russell Simmons's *Krush Groove* movie.

It took us a minute to actually meet. Even though we were on the same tour, we were doing different sets and we didn't cross paths for the first couple of months. And Chad was a little worried when he found out I was on the tour. I was with Fresh Fest well before Chad joined us, but he didn't know about me when he signed up. Being the only kid rapper on the New York scene, he wasn't sure if he was ready to share the attention with another preteen mascot. But he was cool as soon as he realized I was just a dancer and I wouldn't be stepping on his toes!

When we finally met, we clicked right away. Since he was eight years old, Chad always hung out with older guys, rappers, because he was performing. I was the first kid his own age who liked the same things. We could see the big picture in each other. Being everyone's little brothers on the tour was a wave we could ride out together as long as possible and milk for all it was worth! Nowadays I'm so proud to see Chad's a big A&R executive at Sony. We're gonna team up together again and start an artist management company someday real soon.

Me and Chad were double trouble back in the day. On tour, we used to get away from our chaperones—Aunt Lucy and Chad's mom—with the aid of Dice, Whodini's road manager. Dice loved us to death and knew we wanted to get out of the hotel room and see stuff, so he became our enabler. We couldn't believe what the girls were willing to do. Sexy older women in fishnets were actually interested in a couple of 13-year-old boys. We got caught out a couple of times messing around in the back stairwells of hotels. I guess you could say we lost our innocence at a very young age. Technically speaking, what those girls were doing with us was statutory rape, but me and Chad approved!

On the flip side, we were exposed to the bad stuff artists go through living that lifestyle. We watched up close as some of our heroes went through it with weed, cocaine, and alcohol. They respected the boundaries of us just being kids and tried not to use or trip out when we were around, but sometimes they couldn't help themselves, and we saw a lot. Instead of hurting us, it was the reason why we never got into the drug culture ourselves. Me and Chad would just look at each other when we saw a rapper doing that to himself. We never talked about it. We just knew we wouldn't be traveling down that path.

By the end of our first tour, my dad had a brilliant idea. "You boys look so cute together, you should be a rap group," he said. "We'll call it, 'Chad & Jermaine.'" That was fine with us. It meant we'd get to hang out with each other more.

Everything was coming together at once. I was still a kid, but all that touring was giving me the swagger of a grown man. By the second year of the Fresh Fest tour, I was no longer just the opening act. Whodini liked the way I moved so much they started using me in one of their numbers, "Freaks Come Out at Night." I did my lil' thing, break dancing like a demon, and they liked it so much they put me in the video. We filmed on the streets of Baltimore, where the tour was passing through.

That number got me some of the right kind of attention. Record executive Barry Weiss was so impressed with my moves, he wanted to sign me to Jive Records but my dad passed on the deal. I never knew why. Then Otis Redding Jr. offered to produce a record with me and Chad. Instead, my dad decided he wanted us on a small label he created, called the Rock.

I figured I should stay with Chad and his mom in Brooklyn that summer of '85. I guess my idea was to put our heads together and start writing some songs for our new act, but mainly I just wanted to kick it with my new friend. Musically we discussed a few things, but mostly I just soaked up some of the culture that was there in the streets of New York. I don't recall us getting much work done!

Chad's mother had a big brownstone house on Eastern Parkway in Crown Heights, right in the very heart of the hip-hop scene at the time. All day and most of the night me and Chad used to roam around the neighborhood between Bedford Stuyvesant and Crown Heights. We'd go get our haircuts near the Fort Greene projects and just walk around the streets all day, checking out the scene. The big guys knew Chad from rapping contests in the neighborhood, so even though we were just a couple of kids we had access to whatever was going on.

That's when I learned the real culture of rap on its home turf. Hip hop was still just coming out of the projects in those days. Compared to what we kids in Atlanta were doing, New York City was on a whole other level. Chad was the first guy who introduced me to break beats. That summer I learned who Jay-Z was. Fresh Gordon and Big Daddy Kane—Chad was connected to all of them. As a teenager, he was already a veteran of the whole scene. He even opened up for Kurtis Blow when Run from Run-DMC was just his DJ. Seeing what the kids were into and how New York flowed was critical to my development as an artist and producer.

Coming from the South, it was a whole new world to me. I was just a country boy. My house on Judy Lane was surrounded by woods and farmland. But going to a big city like New York didn't faze me. Me and Chad were free to explore every happening street corner without any meddling from grown-ups. We had no problem riding into Manhattan on the subway by ourselves. We hit Tower Records, cruised Times Square, and raided Dapper Dan's in Harlem for those fly shell suits we wore back in the day.

I still get a kick out of coming to New York. The energy there is crazy. It's just too bad that for the past couple of years, my trips there were all about getting stuck in meetings at Virgin's headquarters. New York's become associated with having to sit through endless bullshit meetings with other executives when I could be getting some real work done back home in my studio. But I loved the Big Apple in the late eighties before it got cleaned up. That's where I found my swagger. It became a big part of who I was.

I never ran into any real trouble when I was there. The problems came when I got back home wearing new gear the kids in Atlanta didn't have access to. Chad still laughs about my little look when he first met up with me. I had on the MC Hammer pants, Reebok high-tops and wore my hair in Jheri curl like Turbo the kid from the movie *Breakin'*. But in New York, my style evolved and soon I was all about being fresh to death. We couldn't afford nice jewelry and watches, but we were styling like all the big dudes on the rap scene.

Back in the ATL, there were certain neighborhoods where wearing nice clothes attracted the wrong kind of attention. One time on the train going to Buckhead, some kids tried to rob me. They wanted my new blue sheepskin jacket. I talked my way out of it. There were five of them so I said, "What y'all gonna do, share it?"

A few weeks after my stay in Brooklyn, Chad came down to stay with me and my mom at our house in College Park. It was time for us to start recording so we needed to be in Atlanta where my dad had his little network of sound engineers and drummers to work with us. I repaid Chad's hospitality by introducing him to the country life of riding in farmers' fields in my dune buggy and getting us run off the road. But we also had work to do.

We had all kinds of crazy ideas about what we were gonna record on our demo. The weeks leading up to Chad's visit he was staying in Virginia, so we talked on the phone every day, playing each other old 45s we'd found. "Listen to this," one of us would say. "We can chop it up and use it this way." But we were just kids and the adults didn't want to listen to us. It wouldn't be the first time I'd feel frustrated because I wasn't being taken seriously by older people.

Our duo act went nowhere. The LP we made, and my dad's label, both bombed. Back then I didn't have someone to guide me. But I was cool. As much as I loved break dancing, my heart wasn't really into being a rap star myself. I was already deep enough into that world and from my vantage point, pulling the strings behind the scenes seemed much more interesting. I loved it that, a year later, all the same ideas me and Chad came up with were coming out on hit records by artists like Salt-N-Pepa and Big Daddy Kane. Our instincts were right. We knew the kind of music we wanted to do was what people wanted to hear. It was the first big boost to my confidence as a budding producer.

Meanwhile, my connection to Whodini was about to take me in a whole other direction. The guys in that group had some hot-looking girlfriends from Atlanta. Conveniently, they decided to adopt me as their lil' brother while we were still on tour. I was only 13 and they were about 17 when I first met them, but I knew how to charm the ladies into driving me around the different cities where we stopped. It was just a friendship, but they were another reason behind my developing a taste for older women!

Those girls could rap. There was something about them, a spark. I don't know why, but for some reason my mind just clicked and I decided that I was going to turn them into a girl group and produce their record. We called them Silk Tymes Leather.

I already had some experience making mixtapes. I learned how to spin, sample, and scratch by working with Chad and studying Fresh Fest guys like Grandmaster Dee and the Great

Jam Master. By instinct, I seemed to know what records to sample to get the best sound. I bought a cheap drum machine, which cost me $200 on layaway, added my own beats, and became the MC. Those tapes always sold out around the neighborhood so I guess you could say I had a flair for production. Somehow I just knew I should try with real live artists.

No one my age was interested in producing. This was long before the Diddies of the world. Nowadays, a young artist makes one album and decides he's going to produce on the side like it's the next step on the ladder. But back when I started, people wanted to be up front and center. Not me. I watched the early hip-hop producers, like Marley Marl and Hurby "Luv Bug" Azor, and followed their discographies in all the music trades with the same dedication as other kids my age who would read comic books or teen rags like *Right On!*

To me, Teddy Riley is a musical genius. He's been producing for the rapping greats—Heavy D, Doug E. Fresh—since the eighties. He's the guy who first figured out how to fuse together R&B and hip hop. He called the sound "New Jack Swing." That's the sound I was paying attention to when I was coming up.

I couldn't wait to see what he'd turn out next. Somehow I understood exactly what those old-school hip-hop producers were doing and why. It was what I wanted to be. Producers wouldn't become celebrities until at least a decade later, but I didn't care about that. It's always been my way to go in the opposite direction of everyone else.

At that point, I'd never worked in a recording studio. I didn't even know what a sound board looked like. I was just a teenager. But I knew how to hustle and worked whatever connections I had. Eddie Irons, my dad's drummer friend from Brick who I used to watch play when I was a toddler, agreed to help me make beats on his fancy sound equipment in exchange for a production credit.

I came with it. I had the lyrics for Silk Tymes Leather all prepared and I knew exactly how I wanted the group to sound. Eddie figured he was just doing his friend's kid a favor, but before he knew it I took over. At the end of the day, it doesn't matter if you're just a kid and the other guy is full-grown. If you're the one with the road map, the others have to follow.

But Eddie was cool about it. Watching him work the machines in the studio was the kind of education I was looking for. I filed the information away for future reference. When we finished, I had a demo tape that was almost perfect.

The Fresh Fest tour got me some industry connections I made full use of. It was at this point, I decided how So So Def was gonna operate: I'd produce the album and my father would make the deals. Through him, the Silk Tymes girls got a developmental deal on Geffen Records. They didn't entirely trust me to do a whole record all on my own, so they put me together with Joe "the Butcher" Nicolo, a production engineer and one of the partners at Ruff House who was supposed to act as my guiding post.

They sent me to Philly where Ruff House was based and I

went to work with Joe. He didn't get in my way on the creative side, and technically he was a big help. Back then, we didn't have digital equipment like today. It was all analog. He had to cut and splice the tape once I'd laid down the vocals, melodies, and beats. It worked kinda like a film editor who gets his hands on the director's cut. It was the first time I learned a real appreciation for what my sound engineers do for me.

When we put out the album, *It Ain't Where Ya From . . . It's Where Ya At*, things didn't exactly blow up. We squeaked into the *Billboard* 100. But I was just getting started! I invested some of my lil' stack in a few new pieces of recording equipment. There was hardly room in my bedroom for my bed, but I rarely used it anyway. Sleeping was beside the point.

# 4

# LIL' BOYS IN DA HOOD

Toward the end of my Fresh Fest days, I started spending more time at home. By then we'd already moved from the Dhorage apartments to the small house on Judy Lane. I didn't go back to school. They tried to put me in a class at junior high, but I hated it. I was used to my freedom, and the teachers were only too happy to let me leave. Everyone in school knew I was in the "Freaks Come Out" video. It caused too much commotion when I showed up for class. Not realizing what she was getting into, my mother agreed to home-school me.

I didn't really feel like I was missing out on the whole high school experience. I had way too much going on inside the 8' x 10' walls of my room at home. There were my nine dogs and a cat to keep me company. My favorite animal, Mr. T, was a Doberman mix and one vicious motha who we kept around for protection. He'd show off his fangs to everyone but me and my mom.

She was hardly ever home because of all the jobs she had to do, but the isolation didn't bother me. I was a self-contained kid. Even though I liked to have people around, I didn't depend on anybody. When I was by myself, I could go into my lil' zone. That's when I really got into making mixtapes. Alone in my room, all I did was experiment with sounds and beats. Once I started, the hours would pass and it'd be well past midnight before I knew it. To let her rest and give her a quick break from the loud music, I usually stopped when my mom came home from her nursing shift at 6 A.M.

It was late in 1985, around the same time I was home on a break from Fresh Fest and a couple of years before I started dealing with Silk Tymes Leather, when I met my best friend, Eddie Weathers. His mom had passed a while before in a car crash, so it was just him, his dad, a military veteran, and his two younger sisters Pat and Natasha. The four of them lived in a run-down single-story house on Camp Road, a little more than two miles down the street from my place on Judy Lane. It was the kind of neighborhood where the house next door would furnish the front porch with an old car seat and a broken washing machine. Real country!

Eddie had it in his mind that he wanted to be a rapper. Back in the day, he called himself "Spoonie G," after an old-school rapper MC from Harlem. Eddie could dance. He won all his dance battles at school in Chicago and he was known as the best rapper in and around North Clayton High School. But that was before I moved to the neighborhood.

People figured we'd hate each other because we were both good dancers. I still had plenty of shine on me because that "Freaks" video was out, and I was still doing the occasional show with Whodini. But because I was always home and never in school, it took a minute for me and Eddie to meet. We just kept hearing about each other from other people.

Those other homeboys were just trying to get a beef going between us. Eddie was the most popular dude in his class and he was known as the best dancer in the neighborhood, and I was the newcomer fresh off Fresh Fest who was on TV. I was so serious about dancing, people used to see me roll out a big sheet of linoleum on my driveway to practice my moves. They were always comparing us and telling us we'd hate each other. Then a rumor started up that we were both dating the same girl: Marlow. When I heard that, and found out there was gonna be a school dance, I put the word out I was coming. It was high time I met this Eddie dude.

Everyone was psyched up. They thought there was gonna be a big fight, so they turned up just to see what would happen. But when we finally met I said, "Hey, how you doin'," he smiled back and we just started dancing together and hanging out. We became instant best friends.

There wasn't even any point in doing a dance battle. Our dance skills were too different to compare. I was the break-dancer who could bounce off the walls and Eddie was all about the pop and slide. We decided our styles would be the perfect complement for each other and a great way to impress the girls. We were spinning, breaking, popping, and sliding until two in the morning. I don't even remember what happened to Marlow.

Eddie was feeling pretty isolated himself when we first met. His parents moved them away from all his cousins and aunties and uncles in Chicago. Then his mom died. He felt like he'd been dumped in the middle of nowhere. A sleepy suburb in Atlanta, surrounded by woods, streams, and farmers' fields was hardly a place for a savvy urban kid with aspirations in hip hop.

Eddie's a people person, but for a minute he was by himself, just like me. Eddie's father was always working extra shifts, so it was Eddie's job to help raise his two baby sisters. That feeling of having to grow up fast and make our own way was probably a big reason why we clicked.

Eddie was my connection to what was going on in high school. Through him I got to vicariously experience the social side of high school. Neither of us did much with sports aside from the odd pickup game of basketball or touch football. We couldn't afford all that equipment. But Eddie'd sneak me into sock hops and high school football games. He filled me in on who got together with who at the prom, and hooked me up with all the after parties. His friends were my friends, so I got the social benefits of being in school without having to go to class.

One of those buddies was Daryl Barr, Eddie's main man in high school, who also lived in our neighborhood. The three of us became a crew and we hung out together all over College Park. Those two would come and hang out at my house when they were skipping class, which was almost every day. Mostly, we just wanted to be out and see what was going on. We'd ride for miles on our bikes and explore all the different subdivisions.

We'd be at Wendy's on Old National Highway every other day, grabbing burgers and seeing what was going on. On Friday nights, we hung out outside the Frozen Paradise off Old National, a bar that made frozen drinks like margaritas that the ladies like. We were too young to go inside, so we just sorta cruised and observed all the drama that was going on, like when drunk couples went at it in the parking lot.

A couple of years later, I had my first car accident in the parking lot of Frozen Paradise. With some of the Silk Tymes money, I bought myself a red Cherokee. I was backing out and suddenly saw a fight breaking out right behind me. I reversed so fast that I ended up on top of another car!

On Sunday nights, the big scene for us kids was going to a roller-skating rink where they played all the latest rap records. In the South, skating is a serious business. Social acceptance depends on looking fly and skating with style. My mother used to drive us there, but because all the kids stood outside the front of the rink to see who was coming in and check out everyone's rides, we wouldn't let her take us straight to the door.

Before I had the money to buy her the BMW, my mother's car was a dented, old white '67 Plymouth. When she drove that heap into the entrance of the parking lot, we would duck our heads down so no one could see us. We had her pull up by the exit so we could jump out incognito. Then we swaggered up to the door looking all cool in our white Polo shirts with our collars turned up, like we just stepped out of our limos.

We stayed out of trouble for the most part. I always knew how to get out of the way when other kids started a fight, and none of us was involved in the dope scene. We didn't go near any gangs to speak of. But we had our moments of spilled blood.

Eddie's house was on a corner surrounded by bushes, which were great for hiding. One day we hooked up with a few other kids from the neighborhood and started a rock-throwing fight. My man Daryl clocked me pretty good on the head and I started gushing blood. I put two fingers up and said, "Hold up, hold up, I'm hit, I'm bleeding." Eddie didn't believe me and kept on throwing. I was always lying for the fun of it so he figured I'd hid some ketchup and squirted it on my head at the right moment to fake him out. But I really was messed up. Somebody probably should have called an ambulance but we were so afraid of my mother that Eddie did his best to just clean me up and stop the bleeding.

I couldn't hide the next accident. A bunch of us were outside my house with our bikes doing wheelies when we decided to have an Evil Knievel–style competition to see who could fly the highest off a makeshift ramp. Being the competitive lil' dude I was, I had to back up my bicycle about a block further back than everyone else to get some real speed on it. When I hit the ramp—a piece of plywood propped against some old tires—I went flying. So did my handlebars, which came loose midair! I crash-landed on my face.

Half my eyebrow was left behind on the street. I still have the scar. One whole side of my face and the top of my lip where my moustache used to be was all messed up and bloody. Eddie tried to clean me up again. Then we had to prepare my mother for the sight of her son looking all pulpy and mashed up. I called her at work and said, "I had a little accident, but it's no big deal. Don't worry, I'm fine."

When she got home she flipped. She was so mad. But I was even more scared to tell my father. The next day I was due for a photo shoot for some publicity thing for Whodini and my dad, who took it upon himself to do a little artist management of my budding career at the time, had to cancel. It took a minute before I was photogenic again.

Eddie was more scared of my mother than anyone else. Miss Tina, as he calls her, is just a small thing, and she looks young enough to be my sister, but she was feisty and hot-tempered. The meek young girl who married my father disappeared a long time ago. My mom knew that when I was up to something Eddie was involved somehow, even though it was usually my idea.

He came over one day when me and my mother got into

a nasty fight. Sometimes we even went at it like brother and sister. The argument was almost always over the fact that I was working on my music instead of cutting the grass, or doing the dishes, or getting my homework done. I was hanging out in the yard with Eddie, just kickin' it, and Mom came home cussing and yelling at me, asking why my chores weren't done.

I shrugged and said, "I dunno."

"Did you feed the dogs?" she asked.

"Nah," I said, with an eye roll.

My attitude really set her off. She was gettin' all heated. I didn't like the way she was cursing me out in front of my friend, so I told her to hush her mouth. I was in a bad mood that day because I had a wisdom tooth that was bothering me. It hurt like hell. The pain must've impaired my judgment. My mom went crazy.

"Boy, I'm gonna jack you up," she said. "Ya ass ain't too old to be beat!"

Then she grabbed a broom that was lying by the side of the house, unscrewed the stick, and chased me around the house with it. When she couldn't catch me she threw the thing and it landed with a THWACK, square on the side of my face where I was having the tooth problem. I fell and nearly passed out from the pain.

I said, "You did that on purpose!"

She came rushing over to say she was sorry. She didn't expect to have such perfect aim and she felt bad. But it took a minute before Eddie would come over again when my mother was home. Whenever I invited him over he'd say, "Hell no, I'm staying right here! Your momma's mean!"

Eddie always had my back. He was always on the lookout for my mother's car because she had to pass right by his house to get home to Judy Lane. He was my eyes and ears the same as he is now as my A&R guy, keeping tabs on what's happening musically in the streets and in the clubs. He'd call me and tip me off in case I was doing something I wasn't supposed to, like cribbing the answers from the homeschooling textbooks my mom kept not-very-well hidden in her bedroom. If I was on punishment and not allowed to use my recording equipment, or if I was supposed to get some chore done, I had about a seven-minute warning to make it right.

Most of the time Eddie was over at my place anyway. His dad used to get mad at how much he was there and complain to my mom, because Eddie was supposed to be home looking after his sisters. But we had music business to take care of.

I was first inspired to make dance music when I was on the Fresh Fest tour watching the DJs. As soon as I got the idea in my head, I bought some Maxell cassettes, set up a couple of cheap turntables, and got to work scratching my Afrika Bambaataa, Whitney Houston, and DeBarge records. They still sit in plastic milk crates all over SouthSide, the 14,000-square-foot studio I work from today.

I liked to play the records so loud that I could feel the beat vibrate through the floorboards. I guess it was the dancer in me, because I tried to figure out which beats would make people get up and move. I approached the music like a DJ at a club. You need to feel the rhythm if it's gonna be a hit. Even now, when I go to clubs I watch what the DJ is doing. If he's playing the records faster, I'll push the beats a little on the next record I make. A lot of people don't know how to watch for things like that. It's probably why everyone comes to me to do the remixes for their songs.

Of course, my mom wasn't real pleased with my mixtape methods at the time. More than once she was lying right downstairs on the couch, trying to watch TV or get some sleep after a long nursing shift, while we were sampling records with the speakers cranked up real loud. She'd take a broomstick and bang on the ceiling to make us shut up, but we'd pretend we didn't hear and keep on working until she went to the garage and shut off the power.

It seemed worth the risk of aggravating my mother. Me and Eddie had a thriving enterprise going on. I'd make the tapes and Eddie would take care of the production and distribution, selling out our inventory at North Clayton High School where he was a junior. He even set up a table in the cafeteria.

At first we charged $5 a tape, but we doubled the price when we realized how popular our product was. Our weekly take was as much as $200 each. I spent most of that money on clothes.

Things were popping so much we figured we'd better come up with a name for the business. Then I saw Russell Simmons on the cover of some magazine, drinking champagne and sitting in his Rolls-Royce wearing a hoodie, sneakers, and jeans. I could see my future in that image. I knew Russell's label was called Def Jam. Back in the day, the word "def" stood for everything that was cool. I figured, "Well, Russell's def, he's okay. But, I'm so SO def!"

Each time I made a tape, it was a new chance to experiment. I figured out how to do echoes and other cool sound effects over the records I was mixing. I don't know how I knew which vinyl would sound good, but somehow I already had the beats and sounds in my head. I blew a whole lotta fuses but it was worth it because each tape I made was better than the last.

People ask me how I even knew what to do. But there are some things you can just figure out for yourself that people don't have to tell you if you play at it and stick with it long enough. I guess we're all born with certain instincts and we can be guided by what feels right. People just know stuff. You figure out what to do by doing it until it clicks.

To promote our product, me and Eddie started deejaying at block parties all over College Park. As business picked up, we started trying to find different identities for ourselves. It was around that time that Eddie was calling himself Spoonie G. Later on he came up with the nickname Skeeter Rock and he's stuck with it ever since. I had all kinds of different names as well: DJ Invisible and Invisible MC, because no one at the parties could see me working the turntables.

My whole DJ phase was when I first started experimenting with style. I was always into looking fly, but back then I was obsessed with Slick Rick, the old-school rapper who defined bling way before everyone else caught on. I loved his swagger.

He wore so many chains around his neck that he called it "truck." I loved it when he went on MTV and said stupid shit like, "You want to buy my LP, buy my LP. But you don't have to if you don't want to. I don't care because I'm already paid!"

He was so cocky. His attitude said, "You can't touch me!" But most of all, I loved the wit of his rhymes. "La Di Da Di" is a favorite.

His flow is a rare gift. I don't know of many rappers who keep up his level of rhyming for ten lines, but Slick keeps it up verse after verse!

Young artists today never seem to have heroes and mentors. At least none that they'd admit to. When people ask them who their role model is they say no one, as if every idea they ever had in life came straight from inside themselves. But I always had a few people who went before me to look up to. Aspirations and dreams have to come from somewhere.

My whole character onstage, when I'm tricked out with chains and diamond earrings like headlights—that whole "Money Ain't a Thang" look—was inspired by Slick a long time ago. Back in the day me, Eddie, and Daryl would hang out at my house playing karaoke and I'd do my Slick Rick impersonation, even digging up some gold Christmas rope and pretending it was chains.

I just did it around the house for fun. Eddie found some in his basement, and we cut it up, tied it together with rubber bands, and taped up the ends so they wouldn't fray. Then we stuck the rough ends in the backs of our shirts. We took tin foil and put it on our teeth. I found an old fur coat in some yard sale for my pimped-out Slick Rick look. I even cut out some shirt boards and glued on some glitter to make an eye patch! On one level we were just messing around, but we were also feeding the dream.

I always said that if I was ever going to be an artist myself I'd be Slick Rick. I got my first chance to do something with him when I did a remix of his hit "Sittin' in My Car" in 1995. But I didn't meet him. He was in jail at the time. I told Eddie, "When Slick gets out of jail, I'm gonna work with him."

I finally got my wish a few years later when Slick was a free man again and I invited him to record the song with me on my first album as an artist, *Life in 1472*. Before he came over to my studio, I got all trucked up with my chains—real ones this time—and big diamond earrings. I had a diamond ring on each finger like a set of high-end knuckle dusters.

It was a thrill but also a little sad when I met him that first time. Doing time in prison and facing being deported back to England beat some of the natural cockiness out of the dude. It was appropriate for him to quiet down at that moment in his life, but I had to be the one to tell him, "Yo, man, just do you!" The song, "Fresh," proved he still had it in him. These days I'm pleased to see Slick's got it back. He's older and wiser, but he's returned to the fly, confident person he was in the early days.

Slick was my early inspiration as an artist, but guys like Russell Simmons made me want to own my own company and become a music mogul. Seeing him made me realize it was possible. I wanted it so bad I could almost taste it. It motivated me to work non-stop.

From the mixtape business I'd moved on to production. Silk Tymes Leather was also keeping me and my crew busy full time. I was 16 by the time their album finally dropped. I helped them get discovered and signed to a real record label, Warner Bros. They were making videos and opening for big-name acts like Big Daddy Kane and Heavy D. I took care of their choreography and me and Eddie went on the road with them. Look carefully and you can see us moving around in the background of the music videos we filmed on location in L.A. We're the backup dancers!

We didn't make a whole lot of money by today's standards. I netted something in the five figures. But after years of living off of next to nothing it seemed like a fortune. It didn't take long to spend the proceeds. Me, Eddie, and Daryl did a lot of fine dining to celebrate. A favorite spot was Showcase, off Old National, where we'd order champagne shrimp. We were still too young to drink the real stuff.

I bought clothes and the latest shoes—Air Jordans and Timberlands. But my biggest splurge was that first new truck, the Cherokee. By then I was just old enough to drive; after a lifetime of being so poor, and relying on my mom's old Chevy, being able to afford the car I wanted was the first time I truly felt like I was on the path to success. At $15,000, that jeep was the cheapest car I've ever bought, but driving it made me feel like the richest man in Atlanta. There was no stopping me now!

# 5

# TOTALLY KROSSED OUT

Cocky as I might have been, that first record was what gave me the confidence to make my next move. I tried out my producer skills on another act, Javier and the Str8jackers. It didn't work out. Things don't always blow up on the first try. But that's how you learn exactly what to do for the next time. So when Kris Kross came along, I was ready.

Everyone assumes, and it's been misreported in the press, that I came across Chris Kelly and Chris Smith rapping with perfect flow like they were some ready-made act. If it had gone down like that it might've been less work for me. But the real story is that those two were just hanging out in Greenbriar Mall, shopping for sneakers.

I was there with my Silk Thymes Leather DJ and he was attracting some fans who were asking for autographs. Chris and

Chris were in the crowd, but somehow they just stood out. They were younger than everyone else there, but they strutted up to us like a couple of little men, carrying their shoeboxes for the DJ to sign. They had no trouble getting everyone's attention. With their fade-out afros and multipierced ears, they had their own crazy style. But it was the effect that they had on everyone around them that interested me most. They had that glow.

Chris Kelly was only 11, born in the year Grandmaster Flash first broke out, and Chris Smith was just 10. But they had a way about them that was all grown-up. They were cool and slick with snarls on their small faces, like true children of hip hop. But they also had that cuteness that's commercial in America. They reminded me of me when I was their age, and that was something I knew I could work with.

This business is show business. It's all about people looking at you and making sure people look at you. If you have something that is automatic, that gets people's attention; you've got half your foot through the door. You can have a shitload of talent, but not everyone can be a star just by doing what they do. You need more. You need to be able to make the young girls scream.

What struck me about the Chrises was the way their personalities came through. They came across as tough and knowing, but also innocent. They had grown-up attitude with baby faces. I saw an opportunity and decided to make a move.

"What do y'all do? Are you rappers?" I asked.

"Nah, not really," they answered. "But we can dance."

We had our chat. Even though they never really tried before, I wanted to find out if they even had the desire to rap. I kinda already knew the answer: "Yeah!"

Chris Kelly's mom was with them, and I knew they wouldn't believe I could be the guy to make that happen. At the time, I didn't look much older than they did and I was used to being dismissed as "too young." But they all knew I'd produced my girl group and it was enough to impress their parents. I got their phone numbers.

Chris and Chris both came from good families. Their moms were hardworking and protective. They each had jobs in banks. Chris Kelly, the tougher one of the twosome, was an only child and his dad wasn't on the scene. Chris Smith was one of three kids, and his dad worked in the state prison system. I called their moms that night to make arrangements and get to work on their kids' careers. When the families came over, my mother worked her magic and befriended them so everyone would be comfortable.

It was like those kids were waiting to be discovered ever since they became best friends in the first grade. I saw something in them that I could bring out with some hard work and imagination. But it was going to take awhile.

Meanwhile, my mother practically adopted Chris and Chris. They were over at our house on Judy Lane every weekend. On Saturdays, I'd drive to the barbershop to pick them up after their haircuts and take them home. On Fridays, after Mom was finished with work, we'd all meet for supper at Mick's diner on Peachtree Street.

They were good lil' kids. Did their homework and everything, never dissed their moms. For the most part, they were quiet and did what they were told. But they caught the bug of what I was trying to do and pretty soon they were over at our house on Judy Lane all the time.

They used to get there so early on Saturday mornings, I'd still be in bed. Sometimes, if they couldn't wake me with their knocking at the front door and my mother was still at work on her night shift, they'd climb up to the window of my mom's bedroom and basically break in. Then they'd head down to the kitchen, cook themselves some breakfast, watch TV, and wait 'til I was up and ready to go to work.

The point was to get to know who they were. I take the Berry Gordy Motown view that a true producer has to groom the whole artist. It's not just about the song. When you go for a big hit it's about the whole package. The records have to match up with the way the artist walks, talks, and dresses if the act is gonna have staying power. I'm faster nowadays when I get to the heart of who the artist is. It usually just takes a few days of me hanging out in the clubs with them, but the process is no different from when I first worked with Kris Kross.

I asked them to come up with nicknames, so they called themselves Chris "Mack Daddy" Kelly and Chris "Daddy Mack" Smith. We needed to give an identity to their particular brand of coolness. They were the boys in school who were always macking and getting the girls.

The next piece was their look. You can have the perfect song, and musically you can be great, but so can a lot of artists. I think Justin Timberlake is a talented performer. But he's very ordinary-looking. He could be any skinny white kid from the suburbs of Orlando. You could go to the mall and find another Justin. He doesn't make his style interesting even when he's onstage. To me, he just doesn't look like a star.

Whatever you want to call it, everyone needs a gimmick, that lil' somethin' extra. I know people say, "You got to keep it real," but that's bullshit! This is the entertainment business. Let's get over ourselves and entertain people with a few tricks!

I decided the kids should braid their hair. It wasn't a common look back then, except for a few funky older musicians who sported that look. But they needed more than cornrows. One day we were sitting around my house and Chris Smith came in with an oversize Marithé et François Girbaud pair of overalls. I told him to throw them on backward, just to see.

"Nah," he said. "You stupid!"

"Just try it!" I said. We hit the mall and I wouldn't let Chris Smith change back. I wanted to see how people would react. When I saw how much attention he was getting, I knew we had our look. I figured if anyone could pull off that backwards look, Chris and Chris could, and they did. As soon as their first single dropped they sparked the biggest fashion fad of the year.

That small twist got them into a frame of mind that gave me

something to go with for the album. It was like they were sayin' to the world, "You go right an' we'll go left."

They took the whole idea on board so well, that two years later, when they gave an interview to a *New York Times* reporter, it was like they'd been sporting that same look and attitude their whole lives.

"Kris Kross means up is down, left is right, and the inverse is the adverse," they said. "That's who we are. We do the opposite of what people expect. That's why we wear our clothes this way."

Next came the songs. I wrote, produced, and recorded everything in my lil' room with a secondhand four-track recorder. I spent hours laying down tracks and writing lyrics for them. I played records for them to give an idea of how I wanted them to sound. Then I rapped each song for them onto a demo tape, so they could sing over it line by line to get the timing right. It wasn't that they didn't have innate talent, but I had to cook up their act from scratch and the ingredients were pretty raw.

Their joints couldn't be like the usual thugged-out rap lyrics. Their voices hadn't even changed yet, so everything had to be PG-rated. I needed to invent kiddie rap. They had to be party songs with bounce and flava that could cross over between kids and adults. There was nothing at the time for younger fans of hip hop to listen to—all the albums had warning labels on them—so I knew there was a big gap I could fill. There was definitely money to be made.

To make the point that Kris Kross was one of the first urban acts for young black kids since the Jacksons, I even sampled three keys of a Jackson Five song, "I Want You Back." More than a year later, after they blew up, that reference was partly what landed them a gig as the opening act of Michael Jackson's European tour. Kris Kross also got a spot in his video, "Jam." It was perfect, because since his family broke out, Michael was the next big thing for younger kids to look to in black music.

But all that was later, long before I had any idea of the kind of impact Kris Kross would have. In the beginning, I was just focused on having enough material to put together an album, *Totally Krossed Out*. Building my first album from scratch without anyone to guide me was a process that took all my time and energy to get right. It also took me a minute to get a record deal. In the end, I went back to Joe the Butcher, who had a relationship with Sony through his independent label, Ruff House. He passed the word along to the right people, and helped me put the album out.

It caught fire real fast. I guess it was the first time anyone had put out the kind of hip hop that middle America—and white people—could handle. They were just little harmless kids with crazy clothes who rapped about missing the school bus. But they had enough of an edge that it wasn't all bubblegum. They also rhymed about growing up in the streets, where they were witness to all the goings-on in the 'hood, even shootings.

Kris Kross ignited a craze that went beyond the music. Kids in every mall in America started braiding their hair in cornrows and wearing their hats, tees, and jeans on backwards. For a minute it was like their song "Jump" said, "everything is the back with a little slack, and inside out is wiggida, wiggida, wiggida, wack!"

Next thing I knew, they were on *The Arsenio Hall Show*, the *Today* show, *In Living Color*, *Good Morning America*, *A Current Affair*, *The Tonight Show*, and *The Oprah Winfrey Show*. Everybody wanted a piece of them. When one of the Chrises was being interviewed on the *Tonight Show* his pager went off. When he said it was his mother, the whole audience went crazy. "Aaaaaaaaaaaw" was all I could hear backstage. Everyone wanted to take 'em home!

I never really spoke to any of these media players myself. It's not like anyone pointed me out to Oprah and said, "This is the brains behind Kris Kross; he's someone you should know." I've been on Oprah's couch since, as Janet's boyfriend. But back then I was invisible, like I was Anakin Skywalker in his early years, never taken seriously by the elders. I doubt she'd have cared much about my story anyway.

But I got noticed in a way that counts more. When music publishing execs heard that I'd single-handedly composed the whole record, I became the object of a bidding war. I ended up signing with EMI as one of their songwriters. I picked them because I liked the guy I was dealing with, Steve Prudholme. He was the first person at the corporate level to ever give me any respect and treat me like an adult, even though I was still in my teens. It didn't hurt that he also cut me my first $1 million check as an advance on half my future song royalties. We've been friends ever since.

As record sales continued to skyrocket, I got another $1 million check, this time from Columbia Records. It was money to help me launch So So Def Productions. I could use that stash to find and produce new acts under the So So Def imprint.

My lil' enterprise of mixtapes was growing up to play in the big leagues. Long before Puffy's Bad Boy Records, Murder Inc., and Roc-A-Fella Records, it was one of the first production deals of its kind between a major label and a kid with a start-up independent hip-hop label. Only Def Jam Records could have made a similar claim at the time.

The rewards for all those lean teen years couldn't have come at a better time. I almost lost Eddie to the army. For the past couple of years, his dad kept questioning why Eddie was hanging around helping me with all this music stuff when he wasn't getting paid. I could understand it. Until that point I hadn't found an act that really blew up and there wasn't enough money to support the both of us. But I knew something was right around the corner.

Just a few months before I got that first big check, Eddie started acting kinda funny. I knew it was going to get deep when he came up to me one day to tell me something.

"Yo, man, what's up?" I said.

"J.D., man, I've got to leave, I'm signing up for military duty tomorrow," he said.

"Say, what? Man, you crazy! You gonna end up being sent to Kuwait, and you know it's a mess over there. Don't do it!"

"Bro' I have to," he said. "My dad's right. It's time for me to grow up an' start pullin' a paycheck. I've got my two baby sisters to support as well as myself."

"Eddie I've got your back. Stay!" I pleaded. "It's all gonna pay off, you'll see! Just let this Kris Kross thing take off, then I'll put you on the payroll as my right-hand guy. You gotta believe me when I tell you, this is gonna work!"

Eddie stayed. He knew I needed him. From the beginning he was my eyes and ears on the street and he's always been one of the few people I can trust. He's the people-person who knows everyone in town, but he also knows music and understands better than anyone how I do what I do. Because he's connected to what's going on, he brings a lot of hot new acts to my attention. Losing my homeboy to active duty right before things really started to heat up would have been just too damn sad. We had other more important battles to wage.

It was around that same time, a little before Kris Kross broke, that Ian Burke, a local talent scout, introduced me to some girls: Tionne Watkins, a.k.a. T-Boz, Lisa "Left Eye" Lopes, and Crystal Jones, who was later replaced by Rozonda "Chilli" Thomas.

The group would become known as TLC, but back then they called themselves "Second Nature." They were looking for someone to sign them. Those girls could sing and rap, and they were real easy on the eyes. They had strong identities, like Kris Kross, and they knew how to be trendsetters with their sporty cool-girl look. But musically they didn't really know themselves yet.

When I said I'd work with them, they practically moved in. The little house on Judy Lane was getting to be full of kids 'round the clock. My mom cooked for them and did their laundry while I got to work on helping them lay down vocals in the bedroom that was still serving as my studio.

Later on in their careers, when their personal lives got kinda messed up and the group nearly dissolved, the newspapers and tabloids would write about stuff like Lisa burning down her footballer boyfriend's house and crashing cars. But I always think of them as cool, down-home girls. They were fun to kick it with. They were like kids I'd go to school with, if I ever went to school.

My mother didn't know it, but Left Eye didn't always leave with everybody else at night. She'd moved to Atlanta from Philly just to start her music career, but she was dirt poor and basically homeless. Apart from the other girls in the group, me and Eddie were her only family in Atlanta, so she used to sleep over at my house.

Back then, my mom was pretty strict about me having girls in my room, so when it was time to go, Eddie would pretend to leave with Left Eye. Then my mom would go off to work, and Left Eye would sneak back in. Next morning, right before my mother came home, I'd hide Left Eye in a closet and Eddie would show up and pull her out of the closet while I distracted my mother. Then the two of them would casually come up from behind and say, "Hi Miss Tina," pretending like Left Eye just walked in with him.

T-Boz was also cool. Once she came over to the house she'd stay inside the whole time. She never used to hang out with us outside because she was terrified of the dogs, especially Mr. T! But she was like one of the guys. She'd always play video games with me and squeal at the top of her lungs on the rare occasion she beat my ass. She liked to bet on the games too, which always made things interesting.

But what I liked about her most was her husky speaking voice. As a favor to me she sang on the demo tapes I was making for Kris Kross. But she didn't have that scratchy rough sound when she was singing. I told her she should sing like she talks and hit those low notes.

"Nah, no way," she said. "You stupid! I'll sound like a man and people will think I'm gay!"

"No, I'm telling you it'll be hot!" I said. "It's different, like Jody Watley's song 'Still a Thrill,' remember? No one else is doing that right now Tete! I'm tellin' you, it can be your thing!"

She finally agreed to sing deep on that first demo tape, "I Wanna Get Wit You." When she did, it was the beginning of TLC as we know them today. T-Boz laid down her vocals like I asked her to and finally found her true voice.

"Oh yeah I like this," she said. "It's kinda jammin'."

She's been hittin' those sexy low notes ever since.

That demo got them signed by LaFace Records. It was the beginning of an annoying pattern in the early part of my career of opportunities missed and snapped up by L.A. Reid. But back then, I was so focused on Kris Kross that I couldn't handle more than one act. It didn't even occur to me that I could be working with several of my own artists at once, even though I continued to produce TLC songs long after they signed to LaFace.

Of course, it's no bad thing to have someone of L.A.'s caliber dogging you. It wasn't always fun to have him swoop in and sign hot acts right from under my nose. But it did wake me up and make me realize that I had to pay attention and not get so focused on one single thing. In a funny way L.A. and Babyface taught me lessons even before I met them that fateful day in Alpharetta. Pretty soon I'd teach them a few lessons of my own.

# 6

# MONEY AIN'T A THANG

That first wave of success was a fun ride. The money went fast. A million dollars doesn't last as long as you think it might. In fact, it's wise to hold that big fat check in your hand and stare at it as long as you can, because as soon as you deposit it in your back account it starts to disappear—to the IRS, to the Ralph Lauren store, to the car dealer, or to the real estate broker. I wasted no time acquiring all those things I craved but could never afford.

I rapped about that early baller phase of my life on my second album, *Instructions*, where I rhymed about the lifestyle: linen and cars, private clubs and fancy houses.

I'd been reading the *Robb Report* from the time I was 14. My mom couldn't get me to look at schoolbooks, but I educated myself about all things to do with the high life. I wanted to know everything about all the flyest shit: the six-figure stereos and the eight-figure private jets, the best cigars, the finest wines, and all the latest rich man's toys. I still keep the back issues on a shelf in my game room. I refer to the *Robb Report* when I get my little trinkets for my house. If I go to a lot and they don't have a car I want, I can just pull out a picture from the magazine and point to it, so they can ship my order in.

With my first hit, I could finally afford more than just the cover price of the magazine. That life wasn't just a wild fantasy anymore. Coming up, I couldn't wait for the day I could go into a restaurant and say, "Bring me your finest champagne" and because of the *Robb Report*, I knew exactly what vintage that was. The problem was I still wasn't 21!

But at least we were old enough to drive. You know how you play that game of "That's my car?" When you're dreaming of the ride you'd like to have if only you had the money, you look in the street, in magazines, and on television and say to yourself, "That's my car, that's my car, and that's my car." Me and Eddie used to do that all the time.

My car-collecting itch had been building up for a minute by the time I finally got the chance to scratch it. I went a little crazy. Having a fine ride was the ultimate to me after a lifetime of relying on buses, bikes, and my mother's old car. I was like a man in the desert getting his first taste of fresh, clean, cold water. I just had to indulge! At one point I had 15 cars. I used to like 'em flashy or sporty, like a Bentley or a Porsche, but now I ride high on a big white Hummer, or keep it sleek and simple with a black Range Rover. Lately I've scaled back my car collection to nine.

It wasn't just Atlanta's car dealers who were getting the proceeds of my check. I was also Ralph Lauren's biggest customer. Coming up, I always wanted those sports shirts with the polo ponies on them. I was obsessed, so when I got some cash I made a beeline for the Polo boutique in Buckhead and bought tons. It was the first time I came to realize what discrimination really feels like.

Atlanta wasn't Atlanta back then. There was more prejudice. It wasn't like the store clerks said anything. They didn't have to. It was the fact that I had to wait, and wait, and wait for customer service that never came. I knew they thought this lil' black kid wasn't supposed to be there. But I learned quickly the power of my money, because I would buy out half the store just to show them. Then I'd take my merchandise up to the counter and see the stunned look on the cashier's face. They always took my money, but with one eyebrow raised, like they were thinking maybe I'd robbed a bank or something!

I bought so much Polo stuff I've got shirts at my mother's house from 15 years ago with the tags still on. I've always shopped that way. I go into Gucci or Louis Vuitton on Rodeo Drive and drop thousands of dollars in five minutes. Even today I get funny looks from the store staff. I flash my AmEx black card and get asked to show my driver's license!

When I spend, I do it in bulk. I just point at whatever I like on the display dolls and grab it fast. People tell me I should create my own look, but if someone else has the same outfit on and we're going to the same place and I show up first, they're gonna regret it!

I don't know how these girls like Jessica Simpson do it, always in the spotlight and having to keep up with the speed of life. Their fashion bills gotta be stupid. I wouldn't be caught dead wearing the same suit twice, especially when I'm going to some red carpet event with Janet. I've got rooms full of clothes in all my homes from New York to L.A. Janet complains I've got more clothes, bags, and shoes than she has. Most of them I only wear once and never see again. Some things I never get around to wearing at all.

But forget the clothes. By far my first biggest splurge after I got my check was a new house. Judy Lane was starting to feel kinda cramped with all those artists-in-development hanging around. I found a ranch-style suburban home on Dix-Lee-On Drive in Fayette County for my mom and me that would be perfect.

The house had a pool out back with plenty of room for our dog kennels. There were fireplaces upstairs and downstairs, nice high ceilings, and a whole basement with a separate entrance that would be perfect for fixing up as my studio and living quarters. It had a long driveway for the five cars I'd collected up to that point, with room enough for guest parking, and a big fence with an electric gate for security.

It was a quiet upper-middle-class Atlanta neighborhood of $400,000 homes, a stone's throw from where Evander Holyfield built his sprawling mansion. The neighbors didn't even see us coming! Me and Eddie bought ourselves a pair of four-wheelers for zooming around the fields and along the rivers out back. We must have really pissed people off with all the noise we made.

I didn't really care about the look of the house so much as all the extra room it gave us. It had to be a place where artists could hang out and I could create music. I could finally have my own space. My mom wasn't allowed to be downstairs unless by special permission. I didn't need her to see what some artists get up to during the creative process, like when the Notorious B.I.G. smoked up all that weed with my lil' sister Da Brat in the sound booth. There was so much haze you couldn't even see 'em through the glass!

I fitted out the basement with deep pile black carpet and black suede upholstered furniture like some slick hotel suite in Vegas. The Hard Rock Cafe gave me the idea to do the walls in naturally finished pale wood. I figured that'd be the best way to show off all the gold and platinum records I planned to collect.

I had Phil Tan, a guy I hired to be my sound engineer, install a bunch of state-of-the-art studio equipment in a big space across the hall from my bedroom that used to be a kitchen. That way I could roll out of bed and get to work, or work straight until I was ready to hit the sheets. I loved the fact that I could wake up at 3 A.M. with an idea and just walk across the hall to do something about it.

When I was in my bedroom, everyone knew not to disturb me. Even my mother. Activity in the studio didn't get started until I woke up and opened that door, and no one dared walk down the hallway unless by some prior arrangement because I had a flight to catch or something. My bedroom was my private sanctuary. Chantel Watkins, the woman who co-manages my SouthSide studio nowadays, used to hate when Don Ienner, CEO of Columbia at the time, called me in the morning, because she was the one who had to knock on my bedroom door and wake me up.

I was most proud of the bathroom, which I designed myself with black-veined marble, a glass shower, black fixtures, and thick gray towels monogrammed with "J.D."

But my crib wasn't entirely sophisticated and grown-up. I also built a playroom full of arcade video games, a pool table, a seven-foot-high gumball machine, and a home-entertainment system for watching movies and listening to music. There was Mickey Mouse memorabilia all over the place. I had a mountain of stuffed animals on the floor, framed movie cells on the walls, and a Mickey Mouse rug in my bedroom. I've got the collector's bug. Just like the recording room in my SouthSide studio on the north side of town, every shelf and ledge is stacked with action figures from every sci-fi movie you can think of, especially *Star Wars*.

My place got pretty crowded. At one point I had dozens of artists and studio staff running around that house, along with all the dogs and my mother's two cats.

Then like now, I mixed up work and play. In music, it's all part of the same process and it's something artists who come to me have to get used to. I keep my studio shelves stacked with John Madden NFL, NBA Live, and Knockout Kings to name a few. I'm such a fan they even made me a character in some of these games.

But as soon as I had my new crib all set up, I hardly had any time to spend there. In 1992, the first year Kris Kross really blew up, we were on the road for weeks at a time. All told we were gone for about eight months. Besides touring across the country, we traveled all through Europe to open for Michael Jackson. It felt surreal. We were touring with my childhood idol. In a way, it was like closing the circle from the time my dad first came up with my name.

Not that we got to hang out with him. You don't get props like that when you're just the opening act. It was a whirlwind of security, mobs of screaming fans for Michael outside the hotel and everywhere he went. Kris Kross performed to huge arenas full of tens of thousands of people. It almost made you go numb.

The two Chrises were upset that they never got to kick it with Michael. Not that Michael Jackson is a "kickin' it" kinda guy. When word got to him that the Kris Kross kids were upset he sent them a bunch of presents, but that still didn't satisfy them. Then someone in Michael's crew arranged for them to meet him out at some airport in France and ride with him in his private jet. They waited on the runway for hours, but he never showed up.

I wasn't all that surprised or disappointed. I looked up to

Michael when I danced like him as a kid, but I knew he couldn't let his guard drop and just be a normal guy. He was the biggest star of all time at the peak of his career. I tried to explain to the Chrises that an eccentric music idol doesn't play that way but they were too excited and starstruck to see my point.

I've always been a fan. For the first few years of my career, I'd take a camera with me to capture a moment if I was introduced to a famous person I thought was cool. But I don't need to be with them. I was never interested in hanging out with celebrities unless there was a purpose to it. Being a fan is one thing, but doing a job is another. We were in Europe to work, not get snap happy.

The Middle East was another crazy trip we took that year. The sultan of Brunei flew us there so that Kris Kross could perform at a birthday bash for his son. These days everyone talks about an off-the-hook sixteenth-birthday party where I deejayed for L.A. Reid's son, but he had nothing on this kid.

I thought I was tha shit with my cars and fine clothes. But that experience in Brunei was an eye-opener. Maybe it was because we rolled up with our diamond chains, Gucci bags, and sunglasses that the royal family members decided to teach us a lesson. Next thing we knew, all the wives turned up iced out with huge rocks. Everything in those palaces—there was more than one—was covered in gold.

Each royal home had fleets of hundreds of luxury cars, and several servants for each member of the household. I learned for the first time what it really meant to have everything on a silver platter when the birthday boy's mom called and the butler brought the cell phone out on an actual silver platter.

By the time we got back to Atlanta after all that world-touring I was worried that success was gonna go to the heads of Chris and Chris. My big fear was that they would be less hungry and willing to work to knock it out on the next record. Journalists kept asking me what they were going to do for their sophomore record. Everyone was expecting them to fall off because they came out so strong the first time.

"I don't know how they'll do the second time out," I said. "You've got to be starving to make it big and they might be sitting at the top, full."

I said that in front of the boys. It was meant to let Chris and Chris know they couldn't go soft. But I might as well have been sayin' it to myself. Babyface's words were still ringing in my ears.

I never want to feel like I'm falling off. I've seen too many people get to the point where the riches become all that matters and the only thing they become good at is spending money until it's gone. They fall into that "I'm rich" comfort zone and spend all their time in malls like Phipps Plaza in Buckhead that once upon a time they could never afford to be at. They take it for granted.

That trip to Brunei showed me that money really ain't a thang. I like having it, but if I lose it I can always make more. There's always another opportunity around the corner. The only thing I'm really scared of is losing touch. I know I can't ever go back to where I started and stay there because I came up from next to nothing. But I know I have to return to the streets and clubs to keep my edge and understand what the kids are thinking and listening to. Where I came from got me to where I am now.

Of course, you can't go back to the streets and expect it all to be the same. Those early years with Kris Kross taught me a lot about what my life was going to be like as a semi-celebrity in this business. I had to get me some security. I was already becoming a target for people desperate to get my attention and make it as an artist, and people were constantly coming up with new and disturbing ways to slip me a demo tape.

Usually someone slips something into my CD player when I send my cars into a garage to get cleaned or tuned up. But I'll never forget this one guy. I was driving around Atlanta, on my way to do some radio promotion. When I slowed down at an intersection—because the light was turning red, I heard this loud bang and felt a jolt that just about threw me through a windshield. Someone rear-ended me on purpose! When I got out of the car and turned around I saw the dude coming up to me, all smiles.

"What the . . . ?!" I said.

"Yo man, I'm sorry, but I just had to give you this demo tape. I'm your next hit!"

I took his tape and threw it on the backseat. In hindsight, I kinda respect the hunger in him to make it. That he would go to such desperate lengths is impressive. Of course, I didn't play the demo. I wouldn't be able to listen with an open mind. I was too pissed off! It was lucky for him that my car was just a rental.

A few years later I had another scare after we pulled up outside of a club in Los Angeles. I usually hire a car service when I'm in town, and all the cars look pretty much the same: black SUVs with black tinted windows. But someone must've spotted me because as soon as we stepped out of the car, they opened fire straight through the windshield on the passenger side.

I never got caught up in any gangsta shit but when you make money in this world it can attract the wrong kind of attention sometimes. I haven't traveled without a bodyguard since.

The other price of success is that it brings out the haters. Soon after we first killed the charts reporters were saying stuff like, "Kris Kross better save their money because they're just a passing fad." Later on, when we were getting ready to put out the next album they said, "These kids ain't cute no more. Who cares?"

As a matter of fact, Kris Kross's second effort, Da Bomb, went platinum. It didn't spark a fashion sensation, and the sales weren't as crazy as the first time around, but it expanded the American vocabulary and gave everyone a new way to tell each other when something was very good. Suddenly it seemed everyone was going around saying, "That's da bomb!"

But the Kris Kross momentum was never meant to last forever. Things started to turn before we put out their third album. The two Chrises were starting to hang with a bunch of older people—roadies, managers, whoever. These people drank and smoked pot in front of them, and Chris Kelly picked up some bad habits. Chris Smith was usually pretty quiet, but Chris Kelly spearheaded a rebellion and started picking fights with me. It was sad. I felt like I was a bad parent who'd failed his kids.

Deep down I kinda knew my young duo act had their moment. We made other albums, but they didn't do so well. Their voices were breaking, they were getting all pimply, and they were making that awkward transition from boys to men. It was a confusing time for both Chrises. They couldn't exactly start rapping like tough guys from the 'hood. That cover was already blown. But by then my mind was already working on the next act: Xscape.

My man Ian Burke was the guy who first introduced me to a group of fly women who could really sing. Until recently, Ian was one of the top guys at ASCAP (the American Society of Composers, Authors and Publishers), but he was the one on the scene in Atlanta who discovered the music scene of the early nineties and got acts like Arrested Development and TLC signed. He had a real eye for talent. In fact, he was dead balls on when it came to recognizing a star. He also knew how to network and get a meeting with the right people. But he never really got his due back then. Today he's running his own artist development company in Atlanta, Launch Pad Records.

A couple of months before the first Kris Kross album had even dropped, Ian brought the girls over to sing for me at my eighteenth birthday bash. Kandi Burruss, Tameka Cottle, and two sisters, LaTocha and Tamika, all had voices that could sing lead. They came up singing gospel at church, and had this doo-wop quartet sound that just popped. Three of the girls sang

"Happy Birthday" while another did beat box—making beats with her mouth. They were impressive.

"That's the ghetto En Vogue right there!" I said.

En Vogue was some classy R&B female group the girls were into at the time, so it was the right thing to say. But I meant it. I could see in a second how they could be packaged as sexy soul singers with a harder rap edge. What attracted me from the jump was that these girls had genuine talent. No gimmicks. The first time I heard them I was like, "Are my ears deceiving me because these girls can really sing." They could kick it without any backup. Other people in Atlanta overlooked them, but I heard something special.

The only problem was I still had my hands full with Kris Kross.

"I really like y'all, but there's not much I can do for you now," I said. "Just please be patient and wait for me a minute, then I'll come and get you."

They did the rounds with other producers, but luckily for me no one else got back to them like they promised. When I was finally ready to get them in the studio, I still had their numbers.

Soon they pretty much moved into our new house on Dix-Lee-On. I had so much work to do with them, at all hours of the day and night, that it was just easier that way. My mother got involved too, taking them to get their hair and nails done and helping them pick out clothes at the mall. They looked a lil' rough around the edges and needed some extra polish.

Their first album, *Hummin' Comin' at 'Cha*, went like a breeze. We hung out, played video games and pool, hit the Waffle House for breakfast in the morning and talked about regular stuff. They were homegirls. That time we spent talking shit and vibing together is how I came up with most of their songs. I borrowed from everyday Atlanta slang and phrases. The idea for "Just Kickin' It," one of their biggest hits, was the simplest ever. It just came to me when I called up Kandi and asked them, "What y'all doin'?"

Kandi, who does more songwriting than performing these days, told me a few years later that she copied that style of writing from me.

"You know J.D., I always looked up to you as a songwriter 'cause you know how to keep the songs young and relatable," she said.

It was one of the biggest compliments an artist ever gave me!

In the beginning, the girls were eager and ready to get to work. They took my instructions and didn't question me. The first song was a little slow in the making—it took us two days to record. It wasn't all her fault, but Kandi couldn't get the timing right.

"Kandi baby," I said, "You got white-girl beat."

Luckily by then I'd found Manuel Seal, my So So Def staff producer. I've been working with Manuel since I was 19. He knew how to coach the girls vocally and bring out the best in them. Kandi's been able to sing real fast and stay on top of the beats ever since we trained her up on that first album.

Until he got with me, Manuel was living a quiet life, doing music for local gospel choirs in Gary, Indiana. Then he was spotted by a talent scout and brought down to Atlanta to audition for L.A. Reid. He could play anything: piano, organ, saxophone, guitar, you name it. He's an old school soul and R&B guy who can compose and write lyrics too.

But Manuel wasn't used to the way things worked in the music business. He didn't come with a demo tape, just his talent. So when Bryant Reid, L.A.'s brother, showed up to hear what he could do, Manuel offered to play something on the piano. Bryant said, "Nah, man, sorry. I don't work like that. I can only listen to demos."

Manuel was crushed, so his manager, Jeff Bowens, called me up.

"Man, you gotta meet this guy. He's amazing."

I drove over to the Lenox Hotel where Manuel was staying. When I walked in, he was drawing a crowd playing piano in the lobby. Guests were begging him to perform at their weddings. I signed him up on the spot.

"I know if L.A. could hear you he'd sign you, so I'm gonna grab you first," I said.

Manuel was perfect for working with the Xscape girls to get their vocals and beats right. Whenever an artist needs a lil' extra I put them with him.

After two days that first song was finished, but I wasn't happy. I pulled the girls aside.

"Yo, I wasn't expecting this to take two days to record," I

said. "I can't be working with y'all if it takes more than a day to record!"

"Okay, J.D., we're real sorry," they said. "We promise to work faster on the next song."

They kept their promise and never again took more than a day to record. Little did they know that most other producers don't work that fast, and my expectations were not the norm. But I like things to flow fast. I wanted them to learn to do it my way before they picked up anyone else's bad habits.

Each album we made after that went platinum. Xscape played a big part, but not the only part, in helping me build my relationship with Columbia. Label execs there sweetened my deal and gave me the money to create a full-fledged label with enough staff to handle every aspect of music-making in-house. I finally had enough resources to handle more than a couple of acts at any one time, and So So Def Records was born.

But as Xscape became more successful, they got to be more than a handful. Tocha was arguably the one with the most talent, but she was getting a little out of control. She started picking fights with my mother and it wasn't pretty. One day Tocha barged into my mother's part of the house with a small crew of her buddies. But instead of politely saying, "Hi, Miss Tina" to my mother, and introducing her friends, Tocha just ignored her and helped herself to something in the fridge.

My mother was trippin'.

"Don't you come into my house disrespectin' me!" she said.

"Whateva," Tocha lipped back with that look that makes mothers everywhere go crazy.

"You can't just bring in any 'ole person from the street into MY home!" Mom continued.

"Oh yeah? Well Kris Kross built this house. They put the boat in the water and we the ones paddling it!"

I wished she hadn't said that. It was a bad move. There was no calming my mother down. She shoved Tocha out of the room, and Tocha went downstairs to my studio to grab the other girls, who heard the screaming but had no clue what was going down.

"We leavin'!" Tocha told them. That would've been the end of it, but when Kandi caught a look at the steam coming out of my mother's head she burst out laughing, which only made things worse. The fighting spilled out onto the front lawn and I had to pull my mom away as she tried to swing her fists at the girls over my shoulder.

Things were awkward for a minute after that. I had to make sure Miss Tina wasn't around when the girls came in and out of the house. She was my mom, but there were still more platinum records to be made.

# 7

# ANUTHATANTRUM

As if I didn't have enough estrogen in my life while I was dealing with Xscape, another feisty lil' girl came into my life. She was born Shawntae Harris. But we called her Da Brat.

Brat was one of those kids who got into music through the church. She was in the school band, and every Sunday she'd bring her drums to play along with the gospel choir. She started rhyming when she was 11, to relieve stress and cuss out her very religious mom. Who knew then what kinda filthy mouth that angel face had when she was rappin'?

Brat was a real fan of hip hop. Like me and Eddie, she used to sneak into all the Jack the Rapper conventions when they came through Chicago. She auditioned all over the city to try to be the first female teen rapper star. She battled everywhere and usually won. She almost got signed to be in some group, Camrock, but she was determined to be a solo act instead.

Brat had just finished up high school and was wondering whether she'd ever be able to make a living in the rap game when she saw me and Kris Kross performing on *In Living Color* and said to herself, "That's me! I'm the girl version of Kris Kross." She decided to dress just like them.

Then Kris Kross performed in Chicago and invited kids who thought they could rap up on stage. Everyone took their turn, but Brat turned the air blue an' blew everyone away! She had a sassy, flip-like delivery that was unique. She won $50, and security took her backstage to meet Chris and Chris.

"Yo, we really like the way you rap," they told her. "We're going to tell our producer Jermaine Dupri about you."

"Yeah right, whatever," she said. But they really did bring her to my attention.

A little later on, Kris Kross were invited back to Chicago to appear on *The Oprah Winfrey Show*. Somehow Brat and her friends scored tickets to be in the audience that day. For once the set was hip-hop central with Marky Mark and TLC. Brat fought her way past all the other kids to meet me backstage.

She was real pretty. She had light skin and big almond eyes that gave her an exotic look. But at the same time she kinda reminded me of a cartoon girl with her baggy clothes. Her hair was bunched up in a fuzzy red puffball that peeked through a hole she cut out in her baseball cap, like a hip-hop version Wilma Flintstone. She had a look all her own.

I said, "Hey girl, what's up? What do you do?"

"I rap," she said, with a big 'ole smile. "When can I rap for you?"

"Oh yeah, the Chrises told me about you," I said. "Come to Atlanta."

Her face fell. "Come to Atlanta? I don't got no money! I'm fresh outta high school!"

"You'll figure it out," I said, and gave her my numbers.

She told me later she must have called me 20 times, but I don't remember. I was all caught up in the Kris Kross whirlwind. Then I got involved in Xscape. I was too busy trying to get my new label off the ground with the few million Columbia gave me. I guess you could say I was distracted for a minute.

But Brat was resourceful. Her godsister, Dawn, worked for TWA. Brat got herself a buddy pass on a flight down to Atlanta. She had another friend who worked at the Marriott Marquis downtown, so she had the room hookup. As soon as she landed, she tracked me down on the phone.

"Yo, J.D., we here!" she said.

I came over to the hotel to pick up Brat and Dawn and take them back to my place. Brat ended up staying for awhile.

She was nervous at first. I could tell because she wouldn't stop babbling. I left her playing video games and let her explore my rich kid's paradise in the living room while I took care of some business with one of my sound engineers. Then I called her into the studio to do her thing.

She spat her words out with a kind of fury. Brat was raw,

and her rhymes were so filthy there'd be no avoiding a warning label on her CD cover. But she had an energy I could definitely work with. She came to me with her identity already formed. If I was a girl, I'd be like Brat—the tomboy with style who's cool enough to hang with the guys. She could rhyme and write her own lyrics. I liked the whole package.

But in the beginning she was too eager. Her tough-girl act was just that, because deep inside she was an excited little kid. She reminded me of a pup that still needs to be housebroken. She had to learn to just be quiet, watch, and go with the flow. I wanted to test her to see how much more she could do. I also wanted her to learn the business so that when success came, she'd be ready for it.

After a few days, Brat went back to Chicago to pack up a few of her things and relocate to Atlanta. I still hadn't signed her, but I called her to see if she'd write a verse for "Da Bomb," the song I was working on for the next Kris Kross album. It took her four days to write those lines, but she wanted it to be perfect. It was. She rapped it to me over the phone:

*I'll be coming around the mountain when I come droppin'*
  *da bomb*
*Creepin' up on those* Romper Room *suckas who wanna get*
  *some*
*So feel the wrath of a brat with the Mac pack*
*Walkin' away you're like the bottom of a door mat*
*I didn't gain props cause I was a sucka's daughter*

*I had to earn them droppin' dynamite like Jimmy Walker*
*I can pay Donny Mars in a sticky cage*
*Give me 30-30 half-calibre half-gauge*
*And if you don't know what I'm talkin' about*
*Test me out*

The next day, I flew her back down to Atlanta to record it in my studio. I was ready to start grooming my next star act.

With me that process—known in the industry as "artist development"—is just like it is when you're kickin' it with someone. Without even thinking about it, when you think you're just having fun shooting pool or smoking weed, you pick up stuff by being around certain people and staying in their environment. That's what I wanted Brat to do with me.

Mostly, she'd just hang out with me and Eddie. She really was like a lil' sister. There was nothin' sexual going on. Brat was a tomboy. She was pretty and liked girlie stuff, but she just wanted to be one of the boys. We let her be who she was.

It wasn't unusual when we were working together in the studio that she'd pounce on me and start a wrestling match. It'd get so intense we'd keep going and roll right onto the lawn and into the bushes out back! Sometimes even the Kris Kross boys jumped in. Eddie had to step in and defend me. We'd usually end up covered in bruises and scratches. Brat played rough!

I'd get her back if we caught her sleeping on the sofa with her butt out. I'd rub my hands together until they got real hot, draw my arm back like I was swinging a bat, and, "THWACK!"

on the behind. It was a tradition we had going on at the house. Anyone caught with their ass out had it coming and they couldn't do nothin' about it!

But Brat couldn't come with us everywhere. She used to sulk when we took ourselves off to the clubs and refuse to take her. She was too young, and I didn't want her being exposed to too much too fast. Instead we went to Waffle House on Saturday mornings and hung out at the Nike store, Phipps Plaza, or Greenbriar Mall.

Meantime my mom took to mothering Brat, making her spaghetti and meatballs, treating her to bras at Victoria's Secret. Brat became the daughter she never had. We were all treating her like the Golden Child. And that's exactly what she was used to back home.

On a trip back home to Chicago, a few weeks after I signed her, Brat, who was still calling herself Shawntae, was in a club for someone's birthday party and taking over the joint. Someone said, "Girl, you even dance like a little brat, hoggin' the whole dance floor!"

It wasn't like it was the first time she'd heard it. Whenever she got the best presents or the biggest allowance money, jealous cousins always used to say, "Spoiled brat, make me sick!" But it was the first time it occurred to Brat to actually call herself one. She figured there's a little brat in all of us. Who hasn't whined or had a little fit when they don't get what they want? Brat takes it to the limit though.

When she came back to Atlanta, she couldn't wait to tell me

her idea. But there was a problem. We couldn't legally register the name because other people were calling themselves Brat this and Brat that. So I told her to put "Da" in front, as in "da 'hood Brat." It stuck.

Months later, we were in the mall together shopping when Brat saw a Mickey Mouse watch in the Disney Store and got fixated. "J.D., I *have* to have that watch!" she said. "Can you buy it for me, *please, please*?"

It was an expensive watch, and I didn't see why I should get it for her for no reason. I knew she liked all my Mickey Mouse memorabilia at home and, like any little sister, she wanted everything that I had. But it wasn't like she'd done anything lately that deserved a reward. If anything, I was worried that between me and my mother we were giving her too much. It was the same worry I had since the Kris Kross success. If you aren't hungry enough to earn it in the beginning of your career, just how motivated are you gonna be later on?

"Nah," I said. "Not today."

She continued to beg. I tried some diversion tactics like buying her a cheeseburger, but she kept it up, and the more she talked about that watch the louder she got. I think she was getting frustrated, because we still hadn't gotten down to recording her first album, and she had to wait her turn while I completed projects with Kris Kross and Xscape. But she also knows how to be a complete pain in the ass when she doesn't get what she wants.

"Hold up," I said. "If you shut up for minute I'm gonna give you a surprise."

I went into the Disney Store and made her wait outside. When I came out, I handed her a goofy pair of Mickey Mouse slippers with big ears sticking out from the sides.

She straight up pitched a tantrum. It was like nothin' I'd ever seen before. At least not from a full-grown person. She literally threw herself on the floor, screamin' and cryin' like a baby!

"Whaaaaaaah, whaaaaaah!" she screamed. "J.D., I hate you so much! Whaaaaaah! Why don't you love me? Whaaaaaaah!"

Eddie was with me. Me and Skeeter Rock just both stood there, helpless, while we watched this woman lie on her back, legs kicking and arms waving in the air, wailing her head off. We were sure someone was going to call the cops and have us arrested for spousal abuse or something crazy. Eventually she cried herself out in the way a toddler might get bored with her own tantrum. As soon as she did, we hustled her the hell out of there!

That's when I knew Brat couldn't have chosen a more fitting name for herself.

She could get away with it though. She's always been the favorite of the So So Def family because even when the devil child in her shows up, we know she's all heart. For reasons I'll get into later, she's also the most loyal artist I've ever known.

Her turn finally came in 1994 with *Funkdafied,* the album and the single. As far as songwriting, it was the first time I'd done an album with an artist that was pure 50-50 teamwork. Brat had da flo', and I gave her da funk.

It also was the first time in history that any solo female rap artist went platinum. There've been other women who've taken off faster ever since Brat laid the groundwork. But as far as her rhyming skills went, few can touch her.

There were other firsts with that record I'm proud of. The video we made for the single "Give It To Ya," must've broken records for the number of cameos we hooked up for it. It was the middle of a cold, snowy day in Atlanta, but we got Mary J. Blige, Puffy, TLC, MC Lyte, Keith Murray, and Goody Mob to show up. I played drums. Even Bill Bellamy, the comedian, played a part in the video as the guy parkin' all the fancy cars. It was just one big party at the house.

Biggie was also there. Brat became the first female rapper to ever do a duet with him on the single "Da B Side." It was before he reached the total height of his success, but we already knew he was one of the greats. We became friends when he was still on his come up. Biggie, Brat, and another rapper, Craig Mack, all had singles out at the same time so they were on the tour circuit together. We all got to know each other on the road. I liked Biggie's rhyming skills so much I asked him to record on Brat's album and he obliged by flying out from New York to work in my studio.

The great thing about Biggie was that he was just regular. His songs might be gangsta, but you'd never know it from meeting him in person. Most New York rappers roll deep with at least half a dozen homeboys and bodyguards. Biggie only brought along his manager. That was it!

We surprised each other. I guess my early success and lavish ways were already known in some circles. People just assumed I'd act like some rich asshole.

"Hey, you're a really friendly dude," Biggie said when we first met in 1992. "I thought you were gonna be some stuck-up rich kid!"

Biggie was eager to do the record. But he was in the habit of smoking a lotta weed to get his creative juices flowing. Now unless it's a fine Cuban cigar, I'm not a smoker. Drugs were never my thing. I love to drink when I'm in partying mode, although I've been trying to cut that back lately on account of what too much alcohol does to my waistline. But pot smoke is just par for the course in a recording studio and I've never had a problem with it. Aside from the hard stuff the creative process needs whatever fuel it needs.

But back then my studio was still in my mother's house, and even the baddest rapper couldn't mess with Miss Tina. As soon as she sniffed some chronic coming through the air ducts from the basement she yelled down from the top of the stairs, "Who all's been smokin' weed in my house?!"

Usually, Eddie, Brat, and any member of my production staff who wanted a spliff would sneak it out by the pool. Or, if my mom was lurking outside doing chores, they'd hop on one of my two-wheelers and ride through a field to a lake located in a different subdivision so as not to upset the neighbors. But Biggie was the exception. Even though the smoke got so bad I had to step out of the room for a minute, this was the Notorious B.I.G.

"Leave him alone, Ma!" I yelled up. "Biggie's our guest and he's workin'!"

Being a weed head never affected the man's grind. He didn't write his lyrics down. They were all in his head, and he knocked them out like a pro. Once he was in the recording booth he was on. For the most part, he'd deliver his lines in one take. If something wasn't working, I didn't even have to tell him. He'd just say, "Let me do that again." Redos were almost never needed.

We got to work together one more time, me and Biggie, two years before he was gunned down. Me and Phil Tan, my sound engineer, flew up to New York to do a remix of "Big Poppa." It was another hit.

But the two of us weren't just professional collaborators. Over the years we became close friends. Biggie didn't blow up as fast as Brat and Craig Mack had at first, so he used to call me a lot and ask me what it was I was doing with my artist that was working. It got so we talked all the time, and hung out together whenever we were in the same city.

We were so tight that I was even in the hospital with him on the night he died. We were in Los Angeles together for the Soul Train Awards. The next night we were all out together at a party. When the time came to move on to the next private bash at a house up in the hills, we were outside the nightclub waiting for our cars to show up. Biggie's came first, but I was still waiting for my driver, so Biggie said I should ride with him.

Bob, my head of security, wasn't too crazy about the idea and he let me know. Bob's a cautious guy and he didn't like me to ride anywhere without him in case something happened. I was aware of the beefing surrounding Biggie and his crew, but that stuff was going on outside our friendship, so I didn't hesitate to step inside his truck. But just at that moment, when I had one foot in Biggie's car and one foot on the curb, my own ride showed up. I stepped out and told Biggie I'd catch up with him later.

When I found out he was shot just minutes later I didn't even think about the fact that it could've been me. It was only later when it dawned on me I could've been sitting there next to him when the bullets were flying through his car window. When we got word at the hospital later that night that he'd died, all I could think about was that I'd lost a good friend. I've had friends shot before, but never an artist I'd worked with and gotten close to. It didn't even seem real.

Biggie's murder just tore me up. His large personality and warm nature made it hard to believe his life could be snuffed out just like that. I felt lucky I had the chance to work with him and get to know him the way I did. People hold him up as the ultimate New York rapper, but for me and my crew he'll always have a special connection to the South.

# 8

# EVERY TIME THA' BEAT DROP

By the midnineties, business was booming at So So Def. It was non-stop activity in the studio between Kris Kross, Xscape, Brat, and dozens of outside artists who started coming to me for production and remix work: TLC, Toni Braxton, Run-DMC, Bobby Brown, Whitney Houston, Johnny Gill, El De-Barge, MC Lyte, Aaliyah, Richie Rich, Snoop Dogg, Usher, Aretha Franklin, Mase, Lil' Kim, Rick James, Mariah Carey . . .

So now might be as good a time as any to break from my story and fill you in on what a producer does. Anyone who tells you being a producer can mean only one thing doesn't know shit. Every producer has a different definition of what his role is, and there's no right or wrong.

These days you got people who call themselves producers who are only good at makin' beats. That's the new age. They don't even talk to the artists who do the vocals. Others think producing is turning the knobs to make something sound pretty. Maybe, but that's something a good sound engineer can do. Real producing isn't just about what goes on behind the boards.

I'm more old school. The beats are something I'm good at, but they're only one piece of a whole song. I have a crew of beatmakers I keep on tap who can crank things up with their own brand of beats: No I.D., Kanye West's mentor; Nitti, who produced Young Joc's hit "It's Goin' Down"; Young Juve, who works with Dem Franchize Boyz; and LRoc. These guys are like the modern-day, hip-hop equivalent of session musicians. I tell them what I need and they come up with the right sounds on cue.

But by then, we're only just getting started. Building a track is also about sampling what's already out there. I hear melodies and hooks in my head and I translate them through the keyboards, computers, synthesizers, and drum machines. I layer each lil' sound onto a track and play with it until it sounds "right."

How I get that sound is different from everybody else's way. Like I said, I never started with some tricked-out studio and no one ever really taught me how to manipulate all the machines the "right" way. I must've blown out hundreds of fuses over the years doing stuff I wasn't supposed to do.

Even though I now have a $5 million studio filled with state-of-the-art equipment, my most important machine is an old

MPC-60, which they don't even make anymore. I can edit samples, loop and sequence on this one-machine-does-it-all. It's vintage, lo-fi, and there's been at least a dozen upgraded versions since, but every hit record—Usher, Mariah Carey—came out of that little box.

From the beginning, I kept a crate of vinyl and sampled every favorite, every break beat, every snare, and every kick. I don't know why, I just had to have it all stored on my MPC. I thought I was gonna use them, but mostly I was just trying to study how to make my sound better. I wanted to learn how people got their records to sound the way they sounded, and go from there.

When I was little I used to sit there in my bedroom on Judy Lane and play records produced by Jimmy Jam and Terry Lewis—the S.O.S. band, Human League, and Janet Jackson—over and over again. I did the same with LL Cool J and Run-DMC records, so I could figure out how Rick Rubin got that sound. I used to play records all day and all night. I'd pass out somewhere on the floor with the beats still playin' on the turntable!

I still love those LPs. Old-school hip hop has that rough sound with the deep bass. It comes from that very first drum machine that was ever made, in 1980, the 808. That's what created all the early eighties percussion sound I couldn't get out of my head. Like Sir Mix-a-Lot said, "The 808 kick drum makes the girlies get dumb!"

That old sound is hot again. Crunk and reggaetón brought it

back. But when I was starting out I used to go to other producers with that sound in my head and try to tell them, "This is my little idea." They'd look at me like I was crazy and start telling me what they thought I should want. I got frustrated. "Man, this ain't the way my record's supposed to sound," I said. That's what got me into doing most of it myself.

It has to be a lil' dirty. When I sample, I sample mono, not stereo. Everybody else does it clean, but not me. I don't know why, but it's the way I work. It's like when you write rap rhymes, or even when I'm writing this book. If the English is too clean and perfect, it just doesn't sound real and the kids won't feel it. So when I sample, I take it straight from the sample plug into the headphone jack, crackles 'n' all.

At first, I thought, "this sounds wrong." I was blowing up equipment left and right. But then I started liking it. You can't get locked into the mentality that there's only one way to do things. If you do that as producer you'll never come up with that special sound.

These days I work with the best sound engineers in the business, but they still trip over my methods. Johnny Horesco's been with me for about five years, and it's taken him a minute to wipe that pained look off his face. He likes to track everything nice and crisp, but I like it grimy! A lil' distorted is good. He had to learn to back off and not try to fix things.

The key is knowing how to listen.

My first sound engineer, Phil Tan, understood this from the get-go. In 1992, Phil was working as an assistant at someone else's sound studio, but I was never real happy with the engineer at that place. We were working on a remix for Damian Dame, an early LaFace duo, and it was taking three or four days to get it right. Phil saw my frustration. So one day, he pulled me to the side and asked me to let him mix one of my records. I gave him his chance on TLC's "Baby, Baby, Baby." I figured anyone had to be better than the guy who I was working with. It was worth taking a chance on just some skinny kid who knew next to nothing about hip hop.

Phil came here all by himself from Malaysia when he was 17. His family was so poor he didn't even have his first stereo until he was 14. His parents were real strict Christians, so they wouldn't have approved of the music anyway. But Phil came with a fresh pair of ears. Somehow he had an instant sense of what I was trying to do.

On that session there was no ramp-up time, no drama. We barely talked. He works like I do. He just steps back, hears a track the way it's supposed to be heard, then dresses it up, like a film editor with raw footage who gives all the scenes one seamless flow.

Even though I work with multiple producers and assistants, Phil's one of the few who's allowed to give an opinion when I'm in a studio session. Too many production voices on a record can throw things off and make you lose your vision. I never second-guess myself. I don't want vultures in my ears saying something is whack, or yes-men saying something's hot. I take complete responsibility. I don't like to play it all bossy, but sometimes I have to let my people know who are the Indians and who's the Chief.

Once a demo is ready and Phil or Johnny have done their thing, it's still not ready. It needs that one final test. I have a 2000 sky-blue Benz that sits out in the driveway of my studio and that's where I go to play every new track. I don't drive that car anymore. My assistant Tyrone uses it to run out to the Chick-Fil-A to get me some takeout. But there's something about how music plays in that car. Maybe it has something to do with the $45,000 sound system I had installed! That ride was rebuilt from the inside out so that the acoustics would be perfect. If a record sounds good when I'm sitting in the driver's seat, that's how it's gonna sound when the public buys it. In hip hop, that's how we play our music. If people ain't bouncin' their heads while they're driving and playing your music then you ain't gonna have a hit!

The experience of sitting at the driver's wheel of that car and listening is so necessary for me that I'm planning to take out its engine and move it to a special room inside the studio so I don't have as far to go. These days I'm so busy, every spare minute counts.

But even the sound I make as a producer is just one piece within a piece of the bigger picture. It's not all just about sampling or melodies or making beats. A producer also has to understand the mood and feel of a song and where the artist wants to go. That can either mean building the whole act and their songs up from scratch, like Kris Kross, or just making the artist sound like better versions of themselves.

I come in like an interior decorator, arranging things and saying, "Put this over here and that over there." I'll say to T-Boz, "Just get crunk with it in the beginning," and she'll know I mean start the song off with more energy. And just by making one or two tiny suggestions, it can mean the difference between a good song and a great one.

That's called executive producing. I did that last year on Janet's album, *20 Y.O.* I was collaborating with her longtime producers, Jimmy Jam and Terry Lewis, so I wasn't as hands-on as I usually get.

I grew up on Jim and Terry's beats, so the fact that they were on my project was a thrill. I knew I'd be able to communicate what I wanted because they made the sounds I keep coming back to. I just had to tell them to make those old Human League and S.O.S. beats on Janet's album.

It was a good match. Being a keyboardist, Jimmy Jam is more musical than I am. But when it comes to drum machines, beats and this, that and a third, I had to make him understand.

"Go back to where them beats were," I told him. "That's when the beat was the most important thing, when y'all were makin' those records. That's what we all tryin' to get back to."

It wasn't easy. I never had to give up so much control in the studio like that before, but those were two of the greats and I had nothing but respect for them. At first we had to tread carefully around each other's egos. For a change I had to back off on the songwriting too. With Janet I couldn't dictate, only suggest, because she already knows exactly what she wants.

The whole situation was delicate. Especially considering it was the first time I was actually dating the artist! But in the end it was all on me. I had to step back and see the whole picture, and make sure all the pieces fit the way they were supposed to.

It took me a long time to figure this out. I'm used to being the boss in the studio. But it's part of an executive producer's job to be able to play nice with others. I have to be able to collaborate with other producers, engineers, songwriters, and artists. Failure to master this part of the process is why the music market gets flooded with so many unfocused albums. People get caught up in their own piece and forget the whole.

It's like painting your house. You've got to know what you're doing in the living room downstairs to paint the bedroom upstairs. You're supposed to know what colors you used in the other room. When Jimmy's working, it's my job to go listen to what he's doing. If they set the tone, it's my job to make my tracks sound close—not directly matching, but close enough to where you don't lose the focus. It has to be all one thread.

That's why I like coming in at the end of an outside artist's project to produce the last few songs. I like to see what everyone else has done to understand the mood of the whole album, then take things up a few notches. A song can always be better. I can't turn on the radio without doing some kinda remix in my head. It's an occupational hazard.

But there are also times when I'm the spearhead. When I did "Confessions, Pt. II," "My Boo," and "Burn" for Usher, L.A. Reid played my songs for anyone else who wanted to be a producer on the album, as if to say, "This is where we started." Sometimes it's also fun to be the one who sets the bar.

For me, being a producer is just like being a parent, at least when I'm working with artists I develop from the time they are kids, like Usher, Bow Wow, and Brat. With Kris Kross I did everything. I executive produced their whole careers. I'm the older brother or father figure they come to with all their stuff.

I put way more into making an artist than most producers. For them, it's just about making a record. I can understand why they'd want to keep it at that. Being an image maker takes up a lot of time. It's exhausting, and if you do it right, you don't get the props. You're not supposed to leave your mark on the artist. You have to let them own it.

At first I didn't know how to let go and not be in full control of the artist and the song. But I learned fast that a singer or rapper has to start shaping their own career and stand on their own. They need to evolve from whoever created their image and their song. Once they get in this business and leave the studio, they go on tour and live their lives by themselves. They have to be able to grasp what else is going on and learn from other producers and artists. Then, when they get back to the studio they can weave it all together and take it to the next level.

Other times the artist, like Mariah or Janet, already knows exactly who she is. It's up to the producer to understand them and know how to bring out their best version of themselves. Working with Aretha Franklin opened up a whole other world to me. You just sit there and get starstruck working with a talent like that. She'd ask me if anything was wrong and I didn't want to say anything because she was so dead-on that even when she hit a bad note she still sang 10 times better than any other artist I ever worked with.

Each time, you do something different, because no single artist is the same. Whoever they are, whether some raw kid off the street or a diva like Mariah Carey, there's always gonna be a period of getting up to speed with each other. Unlike other producers, I don't just make up a few tracks and hand them to the artist to record over. Each piece of music is custom-tailored to fit that particular artist. And if that artist doesn't end up using the song, it's not like I keep it on some floppy file to recycle for the next one who comes along. I've got thousands of tracks I never used. I don't like going back over old stuff. I move on. That's because the song has to come from whatever moment an Usher, Chingy, or Mariah is at.

The best songs happen when artists let themselves be vulnerable with me. When they come into my studio it should be like they've come to confession and I'm their priest. My best hits with Monica came from her trusting me. She's always been more of an R&B girl, but last year's hit "Everytime tha' Beat Drop," happened because she let me get crunk with it. It became a snap music anthem. That track was the lead song for her album *The Makings of Me*.

Monica even showed me poems in her diary. It was her way of sharing her innermost thoughts. She also told me about some of the hard knocks in her love life and questioned why her man left her for another woman. It's not like the other woman had more going for her than Monica. She asked herself, "Was it something I did wrong?" That's how we came up with the song, "Why Her?" It was a win because it came from a place that was real. It was all Monica.

A mistake a lot of young producers make is that they want to be a part of the story. But a real producer makes something the artists want to own themselves. For a while, when you're working with them, you become them, and a little piece of you stays in the song in a way that only you know about. It's something that's worked against me. People say I'm underrated because they have no idea I'm behind certain songs. My style is anonymous so the artist can shine.

I used to think that putting out platinum songs would be enough and that all the fame and props would come along like a gift bag. I was doing this before all those celebrity producers, and still people don't know me like that. Other people get looked at for producing one or two songs, but I have to do millions of records to get noticed. I've been left out of a lot. I don't have some sneaker deal. Each time I get passed up for some big Grammy category like producer of the year I figure, "Oh damn, they ain't gonna give me nothing 'til I die."

I'm getting better at building my own brand, but I won't change up how I work. I only recently started adding my MC line, "Y'all know what this is, So So Def," as a way of building up the reputation of our in-house artists, but now everyone expects to hear my voice saying something like that on a track I produce. I oblige them with my vocal signature, but only because it's a way I can brand my production company without compromising the integrity of a song. Putting the artist and the music first is what makes me the kind of producer who will dominate the charts continuously and outlast them all.

When I start producing for someone I don't know well, it's like I'm a journalist interviewing them for a story, except they don't know they're being interviewed. We kick it for a while before we start any kind of writing. The biggest part of this game is to listen not just to your own sounds, but to other people, especially the artist you're working with. I make casual conversation about stuff, whether it be relationships, basketball, or gossip about the industry, just to hear what they have to say about it. It's my lil' way of drawing them out and gauging their mindset.

That came into play last year, the first time I ever did a song with LL Cool J. We met a long time ago, when Rick Rubin first signed him to Def Jam, but we didn't really cross paths much. Although I always respected him as an artist I never really felt like I knew him. He was always smiling, polite, and distant. It was like he was wound up tight. When he flew into Atlanta and came to the studio, I could tell he just wanted to get it done fast and beat it straight back to New York.

I wanted to break the ice, so I invited him to a strip club. Ain't no big deal. We usually go at least once a week, me and my crew. It's a good environment to be in musically, for reasons I'll get into in a minute. I drag most visitors along to the Body

Tap, Magic City, or wherever, just to get them out of their element and see how they react.

I once bought my producer Manuel Seal—Mr. New-Age Fu
Man Chu as we like to call him—10 lap dances in a row, just to
break him down a little and bring him deeper into my environment. I recently took Quincy Jones for the first time. We went
to Magic City, a favorite spot. He really enjoyed himself!

I even tricked T-Boz into going there with me once. She's a
tiny thing, but that girl's got a huge appetite, so I told her we
were going to the Waffle House instead. When she found out
our real destination she was pissed.

"I don't want none of them lesbians coming over and hass-
lin' me," she said.

So I got Bob, a big dude who's my head of security, to guard
her and set her up with a big plate of shrimp while we did our
thing in another booth.

But there was no convincing LL Cool J to come out with us.
I kept asking. I wouldn't let up. Finally, he told me why he
wasn't into it.

"Look J.D., I appreciate the offer but I'm a married man,"
he said. "If I let myself be put in that environment, I'm afraid I'll
slip. It'll be hard to control myself."

That was it! That was the song. That was him. It summed up
LL at that moment in his life. We made "Control Myself" that
night, and he laid down almost all the vocals in one take.

Sometimes artists take a while to understand the process.
They'll show up at the studio and instead of just chillin' and

playing pool, or craps, or shooting hoops in my basketball court, they'll be pacing and wondering when we're going to get to work.

That's what happened when Usher came back to do his second album with me. He was always interrupting my play time. When he came in I said "hey" then slipped off to finish playin' Madden. I was occupied for maybe an hour when he came up, tapped me on the shoulder, made me lose a point and said, "Look man, I came here to work and you're keeping me on ice because you're here playin' video games wit your homeboys!"

I just laughed. I said, "Man, I *am* working!"

Everyone has their own method for making records. Whenever she had to write a song, Left Eye shut herself in the bathroom and wouldn't come out 'til it was finished. I play video games when I'm thinking about the music. When I'm stuck on something and I need to work it out, I don't just stand there in front of my drum machine and scratch my head. Music's not the same thing as accounting. I get outta my head and do something else until it comes to me.

It's not like I'm switched off so much as clearing some space and giving my ideas room to breathe. Shooting at people in Grand Theft Auto or Counter-Strike, or scoring touchdowns in Madden is all part of the process. Usher just didn't know it yet. But like every artist with longevity who's come back to me, he grew to understand and be patient.

I'm so addicted to video games that if there's no one around to play against I find random opponents over the Internet using different screen names like Dupri Style and Anakin Skywalker. I have an *Austin Powers* pinball machine and a foosball table, but I prefer the hi-tech stuff. I used to keep a knee-high robot with video cameras for eyes that I operated by remote control. I pre-recorded some trash talk, and used it to greet people who came by the studio.

I also keep pets at SouthSide. Sweetie, my red African parrot, was the studio mascot for a minute. He talks, so I taught him to say a few nasty words, as well as my trademark, "Y'all know what this is!" But I had to take him to my house because he was biting people. He likes it better at home because there's daylight and more birds to keep him company. For a while I also kept a British bulldog called SouthSide at the studio. I found him in the streets of L.A. (seems I'm always taking home strays). Nowadays I keep him in a kennel at the house on Dix-Lee-On where my mom still lives. The only animals left in my studio are the baby sharks in my fish tank.

It might seem strange to keep pets, toys, and robots in a studio, but all these props help unleash my imagination. Things come together best when I keep it fast and loose. When I write for someone, we start from the beat and build a track. From the track I work with the artist to try to think of what to say. Then I call in Manuel to get a little melody going. Just to layer it some more, I might add some extra percussion to the drums I already put down. That's how it worked for Murphy Lee's hit "Wat Da Hook Gon' Be?"

Once a record gets going it's like water in a fast-moving stream. It'll just evolve into all these different things. If a song takes me more than a day or two to put together, then I throw it out the window. If it takes any longer than necessary it just means it ain't natural. It's supposed to just come to me. That's what God put me here to do. If it takes too much time for me to create a track, then that's not the track I'm supposed to be doing.

Of course, the process changes up depending on the song and the artist. A record always takes longer when the artist wants to be more involved in writing the song, or when they bring other producers into the equation. But when it's just on me, I bang it out.

I do everything. I even do vocals. When I write a song, it's in my head. I don't write anything down. I have to sing it first because that's the only way it can come out. When I do vocals myself it shows the artist how to sing the words as they were intended. It's what we producers call "scratch vocals." Whatever the demo sounds like, that's what we're trying to make the record sound like. So if I sing the hook, the artist has got to sing it as terrible as I have!

I don't just want them to get the timing, when to sing soft or strong, high or low. I want them to understand the emotion behind the words, so a scratch is the easiest way to get all that across. But when it gets to that point I have to make everybody leave the room. My pitch is fine, but I know my limitations. When they hear my nasal voice trying to croon a baby-making song everybody laughs, especially Usher.

The most fun thing about making an album is the way you get to jump into a different life each time. It's like being in someone else's movie, but you get to control the action. You work on seven or eight songs with each project. You have to get deep into at least three topics that touch on the life of the artist. Underneath there's a structure to working with each artist that's more or less the same, but the moments and experiences change up and keep it interesting. Every project has its own special DNA.

When I'm working with Nelly it's real easy. We just act up together. Whether it's shooting hoops, playing a video game, or gambling, he's up for anything. Just to get warmed up on an idea last year we went for a joy ride on the 85 South in his brand new Lamborghini. The stereo was blasting and the top was down. While we were speeding in and out of traffic I almost forgot that two SUVs full of bodyguards were behind us, trying to keep up.

One thing I never did was get drunk to write a song, until I did "Grillz" with Nelly. I was slizzered! It just sort of happened that way.

The whole record took two days. First I made the beat. Nelly came up with a hook. Then we talked about putting Paul Wall—the grill man himself—on the record. We called him in Houston and played some of what we had over the phone to him. He was pumped and ready to be a part of it and told us he'd fly to Atlanta the next day. It was one of those moments when you know right away you have a hit.

Paul Wall was late getting to the studio, so we headed off with our crew to Club 112. A couple hours later, at around 2 in the morning, my engineer called and told us to get back there because Paul had just finished recording his verse. We rushed back to the studio and brought half the club with us to continue the party. We had champagne, vodka, tequila, you name it!

Paul Wall brought his own cocktail mix, something they like down in Texas called "sysurp"—cough medicine mixed with codeine and 7UP. I tried some, and all I remember afterwards is that we kept playing that hook over and over again. Music was blaring and people were laughing and dancing to that same joint until the sun came up! It was everything a great club song is supposed to be: fun, with a crazy beat.

At some point in the small hours of the morning, Paul set up his little grill kit and made plaster molds for anyone who wanted to get themselves a set. Paul has his own diamond and gold grill-making business and does all his own designs. I got myself a $10,000 platinum and diamond grill for my bottom teeth. It sure as hell beats the tinfoil I used in my Slick Rick dress-up days!

Of course, it's rare for something to come together like that in one big party. And it usually takes me a few hours to get my head into the zone before I even start making the music.

That's why I need my environment to be a certain way. I can't stand it when someone comes in and tidies up after me. Like my music, don't make it too clean. Messy means there's stuff going on. There's music being made, so don't mess with my mess!

It may not look like it, but there's order in my chaos and I know where everything is. I like to be in complete control of my work environment. Nothing makes me crazier than not knowing where some noise is coming from. Everything has to stop until I've traced the source. Just the other day one of the cleaning staff was wheeling a cart down the hall and it was like someone was drillin' into my brain! I thought aliens were going to come along and snatch us. Sounds are my domain and I have to be on top of them.

I also need lots of diversions close at hand. If I'm deep into the songwriting part, I don't always want to have to go outside and get in a car for my mental break because it may only take a few minutes before I get an idea and I need to run back into the studio. Because of my little ways I've tricked out my studio with all kinds of amusements to keep me happy, as well as my guests. I have a full-size basketball court that Nelly and his homeboys use when he's in town.

We also keep plenty of porn at SouthSide. I do have female staff working there, but they've got brothers and they're used to the locker-room mentality of producers and artists. Sometimes we play *Girls Gone Wild* videos in the beanbag room—a hallway that joins up the studio and the sound engineers' room. I had it painted up with Pop Art murals of me and some naked blue ladies.

That small annex is where I go sometimes if I need a spot to myself to think and write some lyrics. It's usually real late, around two or three in the morning. It's the best time to get the real work done because that's when everyone's sound asleep and they can't interrupt me. By the time I'm hard at work in the recording studio, you'll usually find a few large guys—the bodyguards—grabbing some sleep on the beanbags and snoring like bears.

The studio also has a living room with a big pool table, but mostly we use it as a surface for rolling dice. I'm a big gambler. I bet all the time, on everything. Horses in the Kentucky Derby, blackjack in Vegas, any kinda sports game, fights, me beating my opponent at pool, craps, or basketball. You name it, it's all worth a wager.

Gambling is how I bond with people. When I first met my man Big Jon Platt, the guy who took over for Steve Prudholme over at EMI Publishing, I ran up a $3,500 tab in wagers!

Once we get started with the dice throwing I can't stop. I'll bet all the cash that's in my pocket and then some. I'll talk shit to people just to keep them betting. I don't like to lose and I won't let anyone walk away from that table until we bet back! Bow Wow claims I owe him more than $8,000 now in unpaid bets. But when people say they want their money I tell them, "Well if you don't have it in your hands it's money you ain't gonna waste in stupid stuff. Bet back!"

It's a running joke that my supposed gambling losses with the studio crew are "So So Def" money. Someone tried to claim the pot was close to $2 million at one point. Ha! I'd never lose that much! But if I don't win it back I pay 'em . . . eventually!

Me and Jay-Z bet on basketball games all the time. One time I lost $15,000 to him. The next week, when he saw me backstage before a performance, the first thing he asked me was, "Where's my money?" I handed him over a fat wad of Benjamins and stood there while he counted. He ended up spraying most of the bills at the audience when he was onstage.

One bet I was only too glad to pay was one I had with Eddie. We'd just finished up Xscape's first album, and I told Eddie, who was my production assistant at the time, there was no way it was gonna go platinum, or even gold.

"I'll be happy if this sells 250,000," I said. "Eddie, what you think?"

"No way J.D., this is gonna go platinum fo' sure," Eddie said. "It's crazy, it's hot! Let's bet!"

"Bet what?" I asked.

"Bet anything. Bet your Beemer," he said.

Eddie had his eye on my car for a long time. He was always borrowing it. It was all tricked out. You could blast the stereo and feel the bass beat through the driver's seat. It was a nice ride.

"If I bet my BMW, what do I get if you lose?" I asked.

"Dawg, you don't gotta worry about that but okay, you won't have to pay me for a year," he said.

A few weeks later I made Eddie my head of A&R. He obviously knew what a hit was. I also handed him my car keys. I wasn't gonna welsh on that bet. Eddie never would've let me forget it if I did.

That must've been the only time in my life I didn't hate to lose. A couple of years back Eddie, Bob, my head of security, Big Al, my other bodyguard, and Derek Dudley, one of the road managers, got into Cee-lo, a game of three six-sided dice that's big in the hip-hop world. We were on a tour stop in San Francisco and the guys were hanging out in my hotel suite when we got the game going. I was the bank. I had a $25,000 stack of bills. But Eddie wanted to bet small. He just had a few twenties in his hand.

"Naw don't bet that, I wanna see some real money!" I said. "Bet five-hundred dollars!"

When you're the bank and you're not afraid to bet big, you tend to win big. Like usual I tore 'em up. I talked trash, like we always do. I said, "Hahahaha, yeee-aah! I'm Mr. Big Stack!" But they weren't having it. They formed themselves a little company they called "The Corporation" and headed downstairs to the ATMs in the lobby to get enough money to match my bets.

When they came back up they had a few thousand in their hands. They cleaned up, took all their money back, ate into about $12,000 of my stack, then got ready to leave.

"Don't pick it up, bet back!" I said.

They had themselves a lil' huddle like a bunch of girls, came back and said, "Now if we don't see the money, we ain't betting."

I laid out another $12,000 in a big pile on the floor and they cleared that out too. They straight ganged up on me an' took me to the cleaners!

"Don't be asking to bet back again," Eddie said, wagging his index finger at me and grinning like a fool. I was mad as hell. I kicked them out of my suite. "Whatever you need, whatever you want, I got you," Eddie kept on, laughin' his head off. "My treat!"

Okay, so strictly speaking shooting dice and playing cards aren't essential activities for the creative process. But I do need to get out of the studio and on the road sometimes. I can't work inside a bubble. I have to be everywhere. Being a producer, I don't just sample music, I sample life.

Music moguls absolutely have to have ears and eyes. You've got to be able to see and hear stuff other people don't, or before other people do. That's a must. As long as I have my ears and my eyes, you can take all the money and toys away from me and I can get it back, and then some.

It gets harder and harder these days just to be out there observing. For a while it felt like I spent my whole day on the phone with Virgin executives. Even though I've since moved on to another label the demands on my time are just as intense. But I still try to be out where it's all happening. Corporate conversations are what my five Sidekicks and my laptop are for.

On a recent visit to Los Angeles, I kept it moving like usual. I passed through every urban radio station and kicked it with the program directors and characters on the radio like Tito, who started out at Power 106 FM as the janitor! I stopped and signed a few autographs for some high school kids who happened to be at one of the stations.

But I never stayed in one spot for more than 15 minutes. Me, Bob, and my assistant Tyrone climbed right back into the black SUV and moved to the next destination, Travis Barker's music studio. Travis is the drummer with blink-182. We had a meeting about my new clothing line, So So Famous.

Then we grabbed some lunch at the Ivy in Santa Monica. We were in and out of there in less than half an hour, because I had to go check out a little store that sold hard-to-find mixtapes on Sunset and see about a new hoodie at Bathing Ape. Then we moved on to Rodeo Drive for a little shopping: five minutes in Louis Vuitton to see if anything caught my eye, and 10 minutes in Gucci to try on a pair of white suede sneakers and pick up some sunglasses.

After that we headed over to the Havana Club, a cigar bar, to meet my man Steve Prudholme. We watched one of the NBA play-off games together. I smoked half a Cohiba, grabbed a snack, and went back across town to the Flyte Tyme studios where Janet, Jimmy, and Terry were laying down some tracks for her album. While I was there, I added a few beats, then did an interview with BET. Then it was time for a quick expedition to some *US Weekly* red carpet event. I did the paparazzi perp walk and answered all the usual questions about my girlfriend. By 2 A.M. I was back at the studio, working.

I spend a lot of time in the back of a car zigzagging across the city to make these stops, but even that time doesn't go to waste. While we roll I'm checking out BET on one of the video monitors, and a heavyweight fight on the other. I'm getting in my phone calls to New York. I'm also scanning all the radio stations to find out what they're listening to on the West Coast.

Meanwhile, I'm talkin' shit with Bob, Tyrone, and our driver, Bobby Earl, usually about basketball. Bobby Earl had the gall to suggest that there were other players who wore Michael Jordan's jersey, number 23, so I spent the rest of the afternoon in the car riding him and making him prove it to me!

A lot of my life-sampling is spontaneous. I rarely plan ahead more than a day at a time unless I'm scheduling some studio time with an artist, and even that can change.

To be a producer, you can't just hole up in the studio. You have to go places, pay attention, and just watch. I learn a lot just by changing it up and putting myself in contact with all kinds. That's why I do my radio show every Saturday night on V-103 FM in Atlanta. Besides using it as a vehicle to promote my own stuff, it gives me a chance to check out what else is hot and introduce up-and-comers to radio. But my favorite part of the show is when listeners call in and tell me what they like. It's my opportunity to talk to the average music fan and check the pulse of the listening public. That's why, no matter where I am or what I'm doing, I never miss a show.

I also go from club to club just to hear what the DJs are playing and which songs get everyone on the dance floor. I wanna know how fast the latest beats are pumping and how deep the bass goes. By the time it hits the radio it's almost too late. The song's already been heard. What's out there on the streets is what's hot!

It's not like it was in the days of Berry Gordy's Motown. Because of the Internet, things change up so fast and kids move on to the next thing before you know it. If you don't get out there and keep on top of what's going on, your music won't be relevant. You've gotta be out there, everywhere, all the time.

Strip clubs are basically a way into that street life. It's always nice to look at, but I'm not really there for the booty. Magic City and the Body Tap are my special music laboratories. These are the places where artists and records break, especially in the South. In strip clubs, the music gets nice and grimy. People can lose their inhibitions so you really get to know how they feel about the music. I'd even say strip airplay is stronger than radio airplay in Atlanta.

A naked woman dancing in front of a customer tends to put that record in a new light. Wanna hit? Watch how she moves those hips when your song comes on. If the girls are requesting the track and shakin' it to the beat you know it's gonna cross over into radio. It's like the girls are hit detectors. That's why guys wanting to get their demos heard try to pay off the strip club DJs to play 'em. They know some cat like me is sitting in the club studying how the ladies and the audience react to their song.

Strip clubs are for real down an' dirty grassroots marketing. Young Jeezy broke in strip clubs. Rick Ross's song "Hustlin" did well—strippers made money off of it. They moved so well, they made their customers happy and got more bills thrown at them.

Mom and Dad, 1972.

Me and my Pop Warner League
uniform, around eight years old.

Me, way back in the day, with my Grandpa
Lee in Asheville, NC.

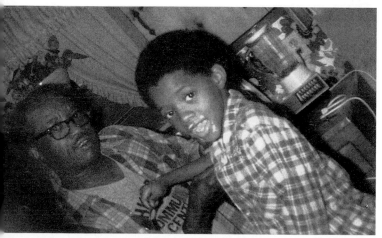

Ricky Bell of Bell Biv DeVoe, T-Boz, and me.

Me, T-Boz and my man Teddy Riley at my birthday party in Atlanta, in 1994.
Back then he performed with the group BlackStreet.

Me and MBA star Allen Iverson, at another one of my birthday parties.

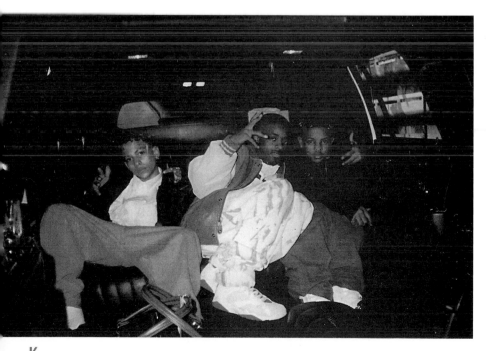

Kris Kross in the early years, globetrotting with me in the days before I had braids.
My Air Jordan 7s look fresh!

Me, about age seven, with my 'hood rock!

My mom.

Me and Bow Wow on his second tour for "Bounce With Me," wearing the paw chain I got him.

Me with Brat and Kris Kross, the original cast of So So Def Records.

Me dressed up for my school picture, back in the day when I went to school . . .

Me and MC, of course.

Me and my man Eddie Weathers showing off our dance moves in the neighborhood.

Judy Lane, where it all started.

Lil' Bow Wow, me, Alicia Keys before she blew up, and Ricky Bell.

Me and my baby girl Shaniah, age two. Our crew is getting ready to do some white-water rafting in North Carolina.

Kris Kross, me and Biggie (center), around 1994 in New York City.

Me and Elton John at one of my birthday bashes in Atlanta. Off camera, my man Nelly was trying to get into the party to introduce himself to me!

Me and my little sister, Da Brat.

(FROM LEFT TO RIGHT)
Me, Lil' Bow Wow, L.A. Reid, Mya, and Ricky Bell.

Me and Chad in Atlanta, on our first photo shoot.

Me and Chad, clownin' backstage and getting ready for a show.

Me and Chad Elliott onstage, year two of Fresh Fest.

Me and Chad Elliott on year two of Fresh Fest, getting a taste of the lifestyle.

Me and Chad Elliott somewhere on tour in Kentucky, checking out our names on a show flyer for the first time.

Taking five from rehearsals, on the road somewhere.

Chad & Jermaine, the rap duo, in the recording studio.

Me, jumping over my broken go-cart in the garage at Judy Lane.

Me with Turbo/Boogaloo Shrimp from the movie *Breakin'*—
backstage in Long Beach at the Fresh Fest.

Me and Chad performing onstage, somewhere.

Me and my man Bow Wow at the mixing board, working on his album.

Me and my birthday girl, Janet.

With Usher at L.A. Reid's wedding.

Hanging out at Southside with Fantasia Barrino, working on her first album.

I'm probably the only top label executive in the world who goes to a strip club at least once a week. Puffy goes once in a while, but you won't see L.A. Reid or Jay-Z in the clubs. But for me it's necessary. That's where I meet people, learn things, and see what's happening in other people's worlds. The clubs are like a gumbo of life. All together in one building you can find the straight white corporate guys listening to rap in their suits, alongside the hardest thugs who killed 10 people. You get NBA guys mixing it up with artists as well as regular dudes. It's my chance to be in the thick of it all.

For me musically, the strip club is equivalent to the whole mixtape scene in New York. You get exposed to records you're never gonna hear on the radio. It's not like I'm going because I'm horny. It doesn't make my dick get hard. I'm not even in that mind-set.

People ask me if Janet gets jealous because I'm always hanging out in the clubs. Nah! She doesn't care. I even took her to Magic City with me one time. It was like a concert. All the girls stopped dancing because they saw her and wanted to be where she was. Y'all see that scene in my video "Gotta Getcha" where Janet was playing a peep-show stripper in a school uniform with me putting money in the slot? She's in on it. She understands what my Body Tap world is all about. Good food, drinks, nakedness and, most importantly, good music.

It's such a big part of my life that I take journalists with me so they can see the lifestyle and understand me better. One time I took a reporter from a music magazine to Body Tap and I bought him a lap dance. He was cool. But he ended up describing the episode in his article as *me* getting the lap dance while I was talking business on my Sidekick at the same time. As if I'd be so unaffected by a girl grindin' her hips on top of me! It made for an interesting detail to his story, but I think the dude wrote it that way because he was married and didn't want to get in trouble with his wife! I didn't care. Janet knows me better than that. But people are funny.

I doubt it'll ever get to the point where you see dudes like Clive Davis or Doug Morris hitting these joints on a regular basis. When I took Quincy it was a one-off, and he was more interested in the girls than what was going on musically! But even some promotion executives at the majors are catching on and hosting parties in these places. They know they can play a full track at a club like Magic and it doesn't just get cut off in a DJ's mix like it would at a regular dance club. In this business nowadays, if you want to find new artists to sign, test something to see if it's any good, or even break a song by an established artist, strip clubs are where it's at.

I have to admit, going to see strippers is a fun way to do business. It's how we get down in Atlanta, Miami, or Houston. Down South, the ladies get butt-ass naked. I'm always working. I never switch off. But when me and Nelly go to Magic City, we have a ball dancing with the girls. There's nothing sleazy about it. To me the dancers are like friends who just happen to be naked. I've seen these girls so many times I know most of them by name. We're all in it together appreciating the same thing: music.

A big part of the fun is a lil' tradition I started called "making rain." I take big stacks of singles and throw them at the dancers. The girls start off wearing a thong, but it soon comes off so there's nowhere you can slip in the bills. That much money wouldn't fit into a pair of panties anyhow. Throwing money at them is the only way you can really show your appreciation in a way that they'll understand.

Sometimes I get carried away with the dollar bills. When we're both in town, me and Nelly raid our safes for Magic City's Magic Mondays. We've been known to spend $10,000 worth of singles each on the girls. The stacks look like cinder blocks. Then we grab handfuls and we throw that shit in the air! We throw it 'til the club closes! It's not making rain, it's making a hurricane!

We felt so bad about our excesses, one time we took the same amount of money and spent it on toys and clothes for kids and personally delivered them to some local foster homes and community centers. It eased the guilt a little, but we still went back to the clubs.

Last summer I threw a party at Masters like nobody'd ever seen. Everyone on the music scene turned up, from Ludacris and T.I. to Lil Jon. We flew our favorite strippers in from all over. We did it for their benefit, in recognition of what they do for us and our music. We had 54 of the country's finest naked ladies on the stage undulating, shaking their humps, and showing us what they could do. One girl from Miami crushed beer cans between her ass cheeks! I don't know how she thought up her lil' gimmick, but we were impressed.

That night was the most rain we ever made on any one occasion. We each contributed to a stack of $100,000, more than enough to help the girls pay a few bills. It was just too bad they didn't see all of it. Some people at Masters, either staff or customers, kept it for themselves.

That same weekend we had a few other blow-out events, but people more or less kept their clothes on. Down South I'm known as the "King of the Parties." I like to see everybody have a great time and get off on my music, so I'm always laying on something. But these aren't parties for the VIP crowd. They're for everybody. It's how I like to give back and stay in the mix. I'm like the unofficial mayor of Atlanta's nightlife.

We hit Club 112 Friday night. Of course the place was heaving. I grabbed the mic, jumped up on the stage and did my thing. Like always in Atlanta though, everything has to shut down at 3 A.M., right when it's just getting going. They're so paranoid here. A random shooting incident in Buckhead in 2003 and city officials have to turn this place into the state of California.

Next day we held a celebrity basketball game—my So So Def team against Nelly's crew. I couldn't play because my knee popped. One of my artists, The Kid Slim, got in some good shots, but Nelly's team won. He likes to play street style so he gets rough. Of course it helped that he recruited a few members of the Indiana Pacers for his side. Believe it or not, we didn't even have a wager on that game. It was strictly for the fans and their families.

That night we had another party, this time with a more formal dress code, in the InterContinental ballroom. But again it was for the kids. I was just there to entertain. When I party, I don't go to some roped-off VIP section. I like to be in the middle of the crowd, taking over the turntables and getting everyone moving on the dance floor.

Some of the young guys who work for me can't hold their liquor. Rufus, one of my assistant producers, always gets crazy when he has a few too many. He's usually pretty quiet. But that night he decided to start taking his clothes off and do his own lil' strip show until the cops put a stop to it!

We had everybody up on the stage—me, Nelly, Johnta Austin, J-Kwon, Bone Crusher, Young Jeezy, you name it—doing our thing. Nelly was lip-synching and making up words to the songs, not realizing the mic was on! Things were pumping and there were more than a thousand people on the dance floor. We went a little over the usual cutoff point, and a policeman had to come up on the stage and ask us to leave. Then Nelly refused to get off the stage!

"The cops want to shut us down! Fuck this! In St. Louis we get down 'til 5 A.M.!" he yelled out to the crowd. "They can't make me leave, 'coz I'm a black man with a mothafuckin' black card that's worth way more than some white man's platinum. I'm gonna hire rooms for y'all so we can continue this upstairs!"

The room was going crazy and everybody was cheering. The poor cop stood there embarrassed, not knowing what to do. Then Nelly felt around in his pocket and whispered to me:

"Yo J.D., I don't have my wallet with me, gimme *your* card." *Haaaaaaaaaaaaa!*

Next day, we hit a pool party in Evander Holyfield's back-yard, but not before I had to get up early and fly to New York to talk to some students about my life as a producer. Except for half an hour on my couch I had no sleep and I was still inebri-ated when I got there. If they have any more questions they can buy my book and read this chapter!

That Sunday night, we wrapped things up with an after party at the Atlanta Peach Ballroom. It was a real shame when things ended with a bang around 2 A.M. We barely sat down when someone tried to grab the chain off DJ Clue. I don't know who it was, maybe the thief, or a guy in his crew, but someone opened fire. All we heard was "*pop, pop, pop, pop, pop . . .*" and we were hustled out of there by our bodyguards. Three people were injured, but not too badly, thankfully.

Of course, the shooting is what everybody focused on the next day in the media. Three years ago, two men were killed in another shooting that happened to have music industry connec-tions, so of course the city council blames the whole hip-hop community for ruining Atlanta. I think that's some seriously messed-up logic. If anything, the music industry is contributing to the local economy and giving poor kids something more to aspire to.

Mayor Shirley Franklin should come and have a conversa-tion with me about it. When something like this happens you don't shut the city down. That's the price you pay for being a city. In New York people get shot all the time, but that's not going to shut the Big Apple down.

The mayor has to ask herself, is Atlanta becoming a big city or is it still the slowpoke-ass town that it used to be? A random shooting just feeds into all that fear about change and progress. It's like the establishment never wants to recognize how important music has been to the culture and economy of Atlanta. Shutting down the clubs early just hurts us, and it sure doesn't stop someone from firing off a gun if they want to.

Maybe it's because Atlanta's old guard hates on rappers. In 2003, when I performed with a couple of my artists at a half-time show for an Atlanta Falcons home game, Arthur Blank, the team owner and Home Depot's founder, called it offensive. Funny, no one seems offended by how much money people like me are bringing to the city. I hope I get a street named after me before he does just to show him!

Right before that party weekend last year, the mayor wanted to give me the keys to the city, but I passed. I want the city council to open up its heart to us with action, not gestures. The sad part is those random acts of violence are not typical of how we play.

Me and my man Ludacris even wrote an anthem for how we party in the city in 2001. We called it, "Welcome to Atlanta."

Down here in the South, we're the good guys. You don't hear about us beefing. That's not a part of our story. People up north used to dis our music because we rap about partying and spending money instead of blowing people's heads off. We just wanna make music and have fun.

And that, y'all, is what it means to be this producer. Now back to my story.

# 9

# A JAGGED ERA

The funny thing about success is that it never feels exactly how you think it will. Your song could get nominated or win a Grammy and it's nice for about a minute, then you ask yourself, "Okay, what now?" In this business, you're only as good as your last record. You have to keep it moving to stay in the game.

The problem is that it's not always a clear lane ahead. You think all the arrows are going to go straight and everything is going to connect with all the i's dotted and the t's crossed. But the reality is there's constantly some kinda glitch or roadblock somewhere. Things never go the way they're supposed to on cue, they only go right when you don't expect it. By then it's probably too late.

By 1996, you might say business was good. I was spending a lot of time up at the Columbia offices in New York, learning what was expected of me at a big label. By then my dad's career managing platinum acts like the Fugees, along with some of my artists, was getting him a lot of credit. The higher-ups were impressed enough to make him executive vice president of a new black music division.

The machine driving that unit was pretty much me and So So Def, and I was delivering plenty enough hits to keep Columbia's boss, Don Ienner happy. I wasn't cranking out a steady stream of new artists, but their caliber was always high. I had Brat, Xscape, and Kris Kross on my roster and everything they released was going platinum. It was a pretty good batting average.

I was earning my $10 million and giving everybody else a big return on their investment. Even though the executives at Columbia and Sony still saw me as a kid, I was a big part of the story of the label's turnaround. After they lost Def Jam, they didn't have anything going on in urban music until I gave them some traction.

But that period seemed more rough than smooth. I wasn't feeling like I was successful. I was dissatisfied with where I was and all I knew was the pressure I was putting on myself. I needed more hot acts to be the kind of hit machine I wanted to be. It still felt like I had a long way to go. The fear in me was deep that I'd lose my edge. It stays with me to this day.

When I get to feeling like that, or when I have to think through something real hard, I start writing. I was never a big talker, so when I have something I need to express it tends to come out of me in the form of lyrics and rhymes. Sometimes, when it goes deep enough, what's on my mind turns into poetry. This is the poem I wrote one time when insecurity was biting my ass:

> *Fightin' for my life,*
> *I wake up in the morning feeling like I'm being cut by a*
> *    knife,*
> *Scared to answer the phone cause I feel it's gonna be*
> *Somebody tellin' me they takin' my life.*
> *When I say that I mean the life*
> *I worked so hard to live,*
> *The life I used to dream about as a kid,*
> *The life I've seen so many people abuse,*
> *The life I've watched so many niggas lose.*
> *It seems like people don't believe I feel pain,*
> *Like everything is lovely,*
> *How could he have a stressful brain?*
> *Lookin' at what I have to go through like it's nothin.'*
> *An' I could have anything I want at the push of a button.*
> *I used to be happy but now I'm not,*
> *Cause these days I'm doin' whateva it takes to keep my spot,*
> *The spot that niggas gave me but hate that I got,*
> *I feel I ain't did shit even tho' I've done a lot,*
> *I feel like I'm cold when I know I'm hot,*
> *I wonder what would happen if I got shot,*
> *BANG!!!!*

*Would radio play all my records?*
*Would I finally see how much I'm respected?*
*Right now I really don't know,*
*Niggas keep tryin' to knock my flow*
*All I'm tryin' to do is have fun an' do it right,*
*But instead I feel like,*
*I'm fightin' for my life.*

That period in my life, just a few months between 1996 and 1997, felt like my least productive ever. I guess every producer goes through a slow period, and those dry spells can afflict people in this business for a lot longer than the eight to nine months it hit me, but to me it felt like a lifetime.

This is a rough and tough business. People are always looking for you to fall, so you gotta be able to stay in the game. That's what I don't like about it. Everyone's gunning for you to take that nosedive. People are ready to count you out the minute you slow down even a little.

It wasn't like I was just sitting on my ass with my face all moped out. I was always working on something: remixes or songs for some of the acts I had already signed. But it freaked me out that I wasn't breaking any new artists. I hated the fact that nothing I saw got me excited. I couldn't sign an act I wasn't in love with. I had to know they were going to go all the way before I would pull the trigger. It's like dating. You don't pop the question until you know for sure she's the one. I was so unsure I went celibate for a minute.

I eased my professional dry spell by putting out compilation records with Lil Jon. I first spotted him when I was 19. Jonathan Smith, a.k.a. Lil Jon, was a DJ I'd seen around for years at the Phoenix nightclub in Atlanta. Even after Kris Kross had come out I was still too young to go in the clubs, but I still had follow-up singles and remixes to promote and I needed to do the circuit of all the clubs around Atlanta. Because of what I'd done with Kris Kross, the Phoenix was one of a handful of establishments around town that was willing to let me in, and Lil Jon was always happy to play my music.

Watching him work over the next couple of years gave me the idea to hook up with him on a more formal basis. I needed an A&R guy for my new label and my hunch was to hire him. I never even knew if he could do the job. He had no idea what A&R was. Most kids didn't know about the business aspect of music back then. But I had a gut feeling he'd be good. He ended up staying with me for the better part of a decade.

Whenever I pick someone I always believe I can turn them into what I want them to be as long as they've got something to work with. I believed someone in an A&R position should have a good ear for music and a sense of what would work in the clubs and I liked the way the crowd at the Phoenix responded to Lil Jon and the music he played. I just wanted him to continue doing what he did. My thinking was I could play him a record and he would be able to tell me straight if it was something he would play in his club. That's all I thought A&R was anyhow. Of course there's a little more to it than that, but fundamentally I was right.

Later on Lil Jon came to me with the idea to put out club compilations. That was cool with me. My dad always said I should do remixes, and I was getting asked to do it a lot on other people's albums. My whole sonic style, whether it's for an original song or a remixed track, traces back to those days on Judy Lane when I'd layer on different beats and sounds.

People from outside labels started coming to me for remixes of their singles, and it wasn't unusual for the remix to do better than the original songs. It made perfect sense to exploit the demand and start a little franchise with someone who was on the same page as me musically speaking. Lil Jon always understood the heavy bass beat of my tracks, so I knew he'd come up with the right sound.

I fell back on the compilation thing a lot. It was the first time I ever really relinquished my hands-on control of A&R duties. I left it to Lil Jon, Eddie, and Diane McDonald, my right-hand who runs everything to do with production at So So Def Records to this day. I wanted to see if the three of them could put the bass compilations together on their own. I had to see if my team was doing what I paid them to do.

Not that I was completely hands-off. I still needed something to keep me busy in the studio and escape from the unease that was nagging away at me while I was still looking to sign new acts. Even now, if I'm on the road a lot or dealing with too much corporate bullshit, I take the time to escape behind the boards. It reminds me of what I was put here to do and helps me keep my edge.

The early result of that whole movement initiated by Lil Jon was our Bass All-Stars series of records. Our first compilation, a girl anthem called "My Boo," went platinum. It helped keep a few hits coming during a period that to me, felt short on new talent. It was enough to keep Columbia happy.

During all those years I didn't even realize that Lil Jon was busy branding himself into a whole new act. The guy had some serious side shit going on! He was with me for almost a decade, up until my last days at Columbia, but that whole crunk movement didn't happen until the tail end. I just knew Lil Jon as my remix producer and a hot club DJ, not the King of Crunk.

I did eventually sign him as a producer. I was getting so many orders for remixes that he started doing some for me. It was good to have Lil Jon in my orbit. He energized me. He knew how to bring excitement back into the club. With our records, he brought a special vibe into the studio.

Later on, he went on to create the rock era of rap by using the 808 sound I like so much and making it even louder. It's almost like slam-dancing from the days of British punk rock. It's all about going to the club and getting wild. But not in a violent way. It's a beat that gives people raw energy and pounds through you like a pile driver!

Before crunk came along, kids going to the club were afraid to get their clothes dirty. They didn't want you to waste any water on them. That's still the case in a lot of places, but if you go to a club that's crunk, where tracks by Lil Jon are playing, you're just gonna have to get over the sweat stains on your fresh white tee!

Even though he was right inside my building, I didn't know Lil Jon was developing this whole persona. Off to the side, toward the end of that 10-year period when he was working for me, he came up with all those catch phrases—"Yeeeee-ah, Whaaaa-at, Ok-aaaay"—along with his gold and diamond-encrusted pimp cup, his crunk juice, his grilled-out teeth, and his long dreads. He sat in his office at So So Def and just tried to find his own destination in life.

You could say I started him on his quest to become who he is by giving him those lil' remixes to do. The time he spent with me in the studio influenced him musically. But he found his own road, his own path to make money off of a club movement before anybody else even thought about going there.

Bryan Leach over at TVT Records in New York came along and signed him. People ask me why I didn't sign him myself. Right around the time we parted ways I could see and feel that he wanted to do something. But me and Lil Jon ain't that big on talking. Mostly we communicated by grunts, beats, nods, and laughs so I guess there were a few things left unsaid. It's not like he ever came up to me and asked me to sign him. I had no idea he wanted to be a performer.

Fact is, I don't think his thing would have worked for So So Def at the time. Columbia couldn't have handled what he wanted to do. When he tried to break Usher's "My Boo" remix he wanted to do it for download on MP3s, give it to DJs, and hand out CDs outside the clubs. He was taking this real street-marketing approach. His music was a club and streets movement and people respected it for what it was.

But big music corporations still aren't set up for that. My role was to turn a record over to promotion staff and let them turn it into a big pop or R&B record. Things worked differently back then. Lil Jon was ahead of his time. With him, everything goes back to his roots as a DJ. He was destined to be with an independent label like TVT or Koch that could do things his way.

Me and Lil Jon are still tight though. Watching him, and seeing how he spins all his catch phrases and crunk stuff into a whole string of merchandise, is gratifying. I love it!

These days we come together as producers when a project calls for it, but mostly we just party together all over the world. Last year we even made our first national commercial together for Heineken. That was crazy! The spot aired during the NBA play-offs. They had us on some private jet runway just outside of Los Angeles. We were supposedly betting on who would win a Grammy and I won the wager. The spot showed Lil Jon coming off of his private plane to pay up with a case of Heineken and sneaking one for himself.

I'm never mad when someone who passes through my life has that kind of success. It gives me a thrill. Having Lil Jon on my label as an artist might have been nice, but things happen a certain way for a reason.

But I'm jumping ahead in my story. Back when Lil Jon first started producing for me, I was focused on finding my next star and I was getting impatient. I wanted another act that could catch fire fast. That's what this business is all about—breaking new artists. It was already becoming clear to me that the Kris Kross moment had passed. I needed another male group with the potential of at least four or five good records. They couldn't be cute little boys. This time they had to be young men with some street cred who could cross over between R&B and rap. They had to have staying power.

But in the midnineties there wasn't much out there with the sound and style that could perk my heart and hit me in the same place that Brat, Kris Kross, and Xscape did when I first found them. I've got to feel like it's gonna be big. If I feel it like that, it usually works.

Of course I'm not always right. Ludacris was the one that got away. I always liked him, and the way he got down to it. Before he got big I hired him to do some vocals on the Madden 2000 video game soundtrack I was producing. Electronic Arts wanted someone with the sound of a real rapper character and Ludacris was the best person I could think of. I was into what he was doing and that was my way of letting him know. We worked well together and I thought for a second about signing him, but I just didn't have that feeling.

I think he was too close to home for me at the time. Once again I was looking so hard I couldn't see what was in front of me. Back then, Atlanta wasn't hot and I was afraid he would be too regional for the rest of the world. A lot of labels passed on him at first. He proved us all wrong.

Signing artists who are worth the trouble is one of the hardest things to do in this business. It's a big risk. When you put someone on your label's roster you invest so much time, money, and emotion but there's no guarantee an artist can live up to the pressure.

I knew what that was like. Before Chris and Chris I had my share of flops. Silk Tymes wasn't exactly a chart topper. At the same time I tried my hand at making another rap group, Javier & the Str8jackers. They flopped. But that was back when I could afford to take risks and fail. I had nothing to lose.

This time so much more was riding on making the right decision. My So So Def kids, and the big label breathing down my neck, couldn't see me fail. But I felt like I should have at least two or three artists out at any given time. Back in the day Motown would have had six artists lined up and ready to be put out.

I felt the pressure times 10 because people were expecting the young dude who'd had so much early success to burn out. Or maybe it was because dealing with artists with two or three platinum albums each brought its own set of problems and took away some of the fun. That's the flip side of success. Riding with it is never quite the same as building up a whole new act that can appreciate what you'll do for them.

There were some near misses around that time. I had a lot of hope in Trina Broussard. She had one of those great soul voices that was a gift from God. I thought of her as a long-term artist who could stand on her own. A Houston girl, Trina'd been on the Atlanta scene for a minute singing backup vocals for Bobby Brown, Pebbles, Babyface, Mariah Carey, and Toni Braxton. Her mother was a jazz singer and her daddy played guitar for greats like Stevie Wonder, so great music was in her blood.

She could have been one of those divas. She'd pour her heart out in her voice and she knew how to write songs. But if that was enough to make it in this business, dudes like me could retire. Trina was stubborn as hell. She wouldn't take direction from anyone because she always figured she knew best. She had all that talent but she was never willing to be molded. It always got to the point where I'd throw my hands up in the air and say, "Okay, do whatever you want."

In '97, I picked her to do the demo I sent to Clive Davis for a new Aretha Franklin song because Trina's voice came closer to the Queen of Soul's than anyone I know. Clive went for it, and we started production on Aretha's single "A Rose Is Still a Rose." Me, Phil, and Manuel flew up to Detroit to work with Aretha. I was amazed. Apart from Mariah, it was the first time I ever worked closely with an artist at that level. The whole recording session went like clockwork. It made me realize how far Trina needed to go.

In the end, Trina had one hit single with me, "Inside My Love," on the soundtrack for the movie, *Love Jones*. But Columbia never put out her album. There were too many delays and problems and they washed their hands of her. *Billboard* said it was the best album that was never released.

Meanwhile, Xscape was also getting to be a handful. There were some early warning signs. When Brat joined the fold, they went all snippy. They were sweet to her face the way women can be, but then there were those bitchy looks you couldn't mistake for anything else.

Brat tried to fit in like the eager lil' pet that she was, but she felt the vibe. When they invited her out to the club I ordered her not to go. I didn't want her to get caught up in all that bullshit with the older girls. Brat was sore with me, but after a rough night in the studio I went up to the room where she was staying in our house, flopped on the end of the bed and said, "Please, *please*, when you catch fire like Xscape, be a good girl. Do as you're told!"

LaTocha was arguably the most talented of the four Xscape girls, but she could also be the biggest pain in the ass. It started with her weight issues. She was cute but she was a little on the heavy side, and real self-conscious about it, so she'd clash with the other girls over outfits. She couldn't always wear the things the rest of the group wanted to wear. She hated that some people called her the "big girl" of Xscape.

Even before their third album, the tension got so thick it was hard to be around them all at that same time. One-on-one they were okay, but together they were always at each other's throats. Everyone wanted to be the lead singer and resented when someone else got more lines to sing in a song. When that happened they'd backstab each other and come and bitch to me about it. It got to the point where they all came to the studio or promotional events riding in separate limos. If they wanted to waste their dough like that it was fine with me.

The big blowout came when they were recording their album *Traces of My Lipstick*. Kandi and Tocha kept beefing during rehearsals. Tocha had a lot of songs and it was making Kandi nervous. She thought I was setting Tocha up to do a solo album, and that's definitely what Tocha wanted, but it was never the case. No way! The first two albums there was never one person singing the whole song, there were always at least two people taking turns. I just wanted to try out something different. As far as I was concerned Xscape started as a group and they were gonna stay that way.

But all hell broke loose. Tocha called me to drag me into the feud and complain about Kandi. Kandi called me to bitch about Tocha and whine that she didn't have enough of her own vocals in the songs. That was crazy. It was a group, and the whole point of Xscape when I first signed them was that they fit perfectly together like pieces of a puzzle. By the end, those pieces were layin' all over the floor.

But the problems started before all that. Success was making them self-destruct. Since they couldn't sit face-to-face I had to put them all on a conference call to hash it out.

Tocha said: "J.D. I can't work with her no more!"

Kandi said: "I can't even stand to be in the same room as her!"

I said: "Either it's all of y'all or nothin'! We just won't finish this record."

We were halfway through recording. Kandi was afraid Tocha was gonna pull rank because she had so many songs. I told them they started as a team and they'd better finish that way or I was gonna walk away.

The album went platinum. But it could've gone multi-platinum if they'd taken the trouble to do all the necessary promotion. Sure, they were the "million-dollar girl group." We had a great run. They were nominated as best R&B group for the Soul Train Awards. They could've gone much, much further. I loved those girls. They were cool. But, amongst themselves, there was just too much drama. They'd be the first to admit it.

As if I didn't have enough problems with the women in my professional life, I was also dealing with major tensions on the personal front. I was never one for getting distracted by the booty, but in this business there are always plenty of women around and once in a while I'd fall. Even from the time I was just a kid in the Fresh Fest tour I had an eye for the ladies.

It's not like I was some big-time playa. Apart from the odd fling with a dancer or whoever, I usually had a steady girlfriend. When I was real young I used to see a lil' girl named P.J. I'd ride miles on my bike and risk getting run off the road by trucks on Old National Highway just to see her. A lil' after my Kris Kross days I started seeing a woman named Tiffany.

We'd been together for years but there was always too much fussing and fighting. Unless you're both in the business, it's hard to make a relationship work. A girl just sitting at home while you're doing what you're doing ain't gonna be happy. Her mind just goes crazy. You're just workin' hard, all day and all night and all weekend, and traveling, but they just see what's playing on BET or MTV. They think when you're not with them you're partying, drinking, and fucking all those girls they see in the music videos. They think what they see on the TV is real life. And most of the time it is.

I loved Tiffany, but I didn't know how I could set aside the time to prove it. Music always came first. Apart from posters of sexy women like Janet that I had on the walls in my studio, I never kept pictures of girlfriends. The framed photos on my bedside table were of me and my artists. Any woman who wanted to be in my life would have to accept that the music game was all-consuming. With Tiffany I was getting too much pressure from all sides. We decided to spend some time apart and give ourselves some breathing room. At least I thought we were on a break.

By this time I had plenty going on at So So Def Records to keep myself distracted. Kandi introduced me to an old friend of hers from high school—Richard Wingo, a.k.a. Wingo Dollar.

Kandi remembered Wingo having two groups out of high school and she got it into her head that she wanted to manage her own act and make some extra cash. She called a meeting with Wingo at her crib and told him to put together a demo with the guys he only played with sometimes. She figured this other group was badder and more marketable. She was right.

When she brought them over to my house, they turned off my TV, stood in front of it and started to sing. Not only did they have the right look, they had the right sound.

At the time they called themselves Twin AK. The heart of the group was the twins, Brian "Brasco" Casey and Brandon, who sometimes called himself "Case Dinero." They sang with one other guy, Kyle "Quick" Norman. Like a lot of the acts I worked with over the years—Brat, Xscape, Usher—they were religious and came up singing in a choir. Not just sometimes when their mothers made them go. They were bona fide church boys who all hooked up through some local religious rally. They started rehearsing everyday and doing their "Take 6" kinda thing, performing around local clubs and trying to get a record deal.

They had a New Edition flava and a Dru Hill vibe with a little gospel thrown in. I could see right away they were the perfect package: kinda rough on the outside, but with a smooth solid sound that could cross over and appeal to older soul fans and women, as well as kids into rap.

Of course, they were no picnic. They came to me already formed as an R&B group, but I was trying to make them more hip hop, like a male version of Xscape. I had a lot of back and forth and run-ins with them until we came up with a solution: give them a hip-hop image with an R&B sound.

"That's it," I said. "You'll be like one of those knives that's smooth on one side and serrated on the other."

They liked it. Jagged Edge rocked their new street style. I

gave them a hint of hip hop but let them be themselves musically with their smooth mid-tempo tracks.

I even marketed them like a real rap group. I took them to perform in clubs and had DJ Clue do mixtapes with snippets from their album before it was released. We got the buzz going, and followed up with stickers, posters, and postcards all over the streets.

My tactic paid off. Female R&B dominated the music scene in the mid-nineties, but Jagged went on to lead the era of power soul that's rough around the edges. They weren't the only guys who were hot in the genre at that time. Boyz II Men and Dru Hill were all big back then. Jodeci was doing R&B with a rock-and-roll flavor. But I wanted to tap into a movement then find my own lane by including a harder rap element to the smooth Jagged sound.

Their first album in 1998, *A Jagged Era*, went gold; in 2000, *JE Heartbreak* went platinum; and, in 2001 *Jagged Little Thrill* went multi-platinum.

The ladies loved them. One time me, Jagged, and Brat were all out together riding on a tour bus to some club, and a car full of women pulled alongside us on the freeway. We were driving 70 miles an hour, but they started taking their clothes off and rubbing up against each other butt naked. Even the girl driving stripped and started touching herself. It went on like that for a good three or four miles. Funny thing was, Wingo recognized one of the girls from the church youth choir they belonged to as kids!

The guys were eager to get to work on that first album. In

fact the other two guys—not the twins—were always just happy to be there. But problems always seem to come up when certain artists start believing in all their hype. After that first wave of success the twins got a little weird on me.

The two of them lived in the same house, but they never talked to each other. If they had something to say they'd call their manager to communicate. If you called the house you had to call twice on separate lines, because the brothers wouldn't pass on a message or walk into another room to pass the phone. They'd even drive themselves to the studio separately. One would come in, lay down some tracks, sing his part, and leave. Then the other would show up, hear what his brother did, say it sucked, and refuse to work.

Even though they were close in a way, it was like their minds were always off in different places at different times. You never knew what to expect. It was like they took turns at being nice and being nasty. The whole crazy dynamic meant it'd take me twice as long to produce something. Y'all know how much I hate that!

The first couple of times it happened I was mad. Each of the twins meant a lot to the project. They were the lead. But there I was, just waiting on them, hoping they'd show up. I had to go and find comfort in myself, play my games, and calm down. By the end of a week we'd get it all on track, but then it would happen all over again! After a while, I got used to it. It was just a funny kinda way they had. They've matured, but they still work that way sometimes.

Most of the time it was my sound engineer Phil Tan who would have to bear the brunt. I'd lose patience with them and leave my studio to go off and do something else while they finished recording their vocals. They were supposed to wait for me to get back and listen to their track to make sure it was ready to go, but if I wasn't there for even a second they'd say to Phil:

"We're just gonna go get somethin' to eat, we'll be back in an hour." Then we wouldn't see them again.

They were my first real taste of what it's like to deal with an artistic temperament. They were set in their own lifestyle, like a So So Def version of a rock an' roll star like Axl Rose. You could pretty much expect them to show up late at a performance. They'd refused to fly anywhere, one of many of their lil' quirks. Instead, they insisted on going everywhere by bus.

One time they called their manager and asked him how they could make some more money. He found them two all expenses paid shows to do in Trinidad and Tobago. They could bring their wives and girlfriends, and they'd net $60,000 a performance. It was like a paid vacation in the Caribbean, but they wasn't with it.

Brandon was quoted in a magazine interview somewhere saying he felt conflicted about singing R&B instead of gospel. Like he couldn't be doing God's work because of the style of music he chose. Maybe that was it. They liked the money and fame aspect of their lives as artists, but their hearts had to be into whatever it was they were doing at that moment.

I see Jagged all the time. In fact, I'm getting ready to sign them to a new deal that will bring them back into the So So Def family where they belong. We're warm together, like family. They've grown up a lot. In a funny way the twins needed this time to get to know each other as men.

But I never really understood how anyone could work the way they did, at any age. They've always been a mystery to me. I didn't even try to convince them. I knew I'd be wasting my breath. They wouldn't take instructions from me, and you can only do so much with artists who don't listen, no matter how talented they are. They liked the fame, but they had their own way of dealing with the rest of it.

I'm proud of Jagged. They represent one of So So Def Records' biggest success stories. They came close to my vision of what a great act should be despite their quirks.

By the time they came along, my record label was really starting to take on a life of its own. I had multiple groups with records going platinum. I had a crazy number of employees—as many as 30 at one point. Sony was giving me about $12 million a year to operate So So Def and we were giving them their money's worth.

Diane McDonald was always the heart and soul of the label. I could trust her to run things while I went off and did production projects outside So So Def Records. I was getting requests from all kinds of big labels and building up my roster for So So Def Productions, so I needed my rock more than ever.

My dad found Diane way back at the beginning of Kris Kross when he was running his artist management company out of Miami. She was almost fresh out of college, where she studied sound engineering. My father tried her out as a temp, but she soon proved herself indispensable because she knew how to get things done. You'd never know to look at this quiet, conservative lil' white girl from south Florida that she had it in her to run a hip-hop label. She looks like the kind of person who should be reading books in a library! But Diane's all about the business and I love her for it.

It's just as well I had her in my corner because I was about to get real busy working with my next big star.

# 10

# CONFESSIONS

When you're good at what you do and you keep up the grind long enough there should come a point in your career when you hit a nice, smooth groove. Maybe you haven't reached the pinnacle, but you know that if you keep on doing what you're doing, you'll get there, and that what you do can't be taken away from you.

For a while now I've known that no matter how bad my luck turns, my talent is innate. I can always turn to it to get back on track. It's like Neo in *The Matrix* when he realizes that he's the one with the power. I know now that I know the formula for making hits. It's almost automatic. But just like in the movie, it took me more than a minute to realize it.

Other people seemed to understand what I was capable of before I did. In 1995, I got a call from Sony's boss Tommy

Mottola to come to New York, to do some producing for his wife at the time, Mariah Carey. I never worked with a pop diva before, so I was kinda surprised they wanted me there. I thought my style would be too street for her. But it turns out that having me up there was all her idea.

We first met at a Grammy after party with Kris Kross a few years before. We talked about some kid she and her manager were thinking about signing but it never worked out. One of the Kris Kross guys was crushin' on her at the time and was all excited about meeting her, but that period was a blur for me. Or maybe I just wasn't all that impressed back then.

For a minute Mariah—or MC as I like to call her—had been itching to do something different from the usual safe stuff that her label wanted her to stick with. But every time she suggested some hip-hop guy to work with Tommy said, "No way." He didn't trust some rapper/producer being around his girl. I guess it was part jealousy and part fear that an association like that might hurt her image with her fan base.

Even though Mariah always considered herself to be first and foremost a black woman, everyone at the label was scared of her being too urban. She's far from some 'hood rat, but she's definitely a lil' ghetto and she was tired of being called the "ballad queen."

Whatever reservations he had about his girl going hip hop, for some reason Tommy was okay with me. It probably helped that I was already part of Columbia and he was the CEO of Sony. That basically made him my boss's boss. He already knew from Xscape that I could do crossover R&B stuff, so he was comfortable with my style. He figured I could give his girl a vibe that was new and fresh, but not too off the charts. Or maybe he was fine with it because in his mind I was just a quiet lil' country boy from Atlanta who didn't seem like too much of a threat.

Me and MC knocked out our first song, "Always Be My Baby," at the Hit Factory in New York. At first I didn't even want to speak up when I had an idea about how a song should go. I was way out of my comfort zone. Most of my artists had no idea what to do and were looking to me to tell them, but Mariah sold tens of millions of records and I didn't think she'd take kindly to being bossed by me. On top of it all, our work schedules weren't really meshing.

I'm used to starting late and working through the night. My creative juices usually don't get flowing until after midnight, but on her clock we had to start before noon. When Tommy came by the studio to pick her up and take her to dinner around six we wouldn't see her for the rest of the day. No matter what we were into at the studio, even if I was in the middle of working on some crucial hook, the work had to stop for dinner. It went like that for the whole week we were recording together.

Being a collaborator with someone as big and talented as Mariah was something totally new to me. I couldn't find my voice in that situation because my confidence still had to kick in. Then Mariah kinda corrected me. She told me my silence was bugging her out. She needed me to be me and assert myself.

"Look, I didn't ask you up here to nod and smile and say 'yeah' all the time," she said. "If you've got something to say, say it!"

That girl expanded my mind. Once I knew what she wanted from me, it was nothing less than a full partnership. We bounced ideas back and forth. When we were exploring an idea together and something really clicked, we'd both look up at each other at the same time. We just knew.

MC knew exactly what she wanted and what she needed to take from me, and she worked fast. Once we were ready to record, it almost never took more than one take to get it right, and if I needed a redo I didn't even have to tell her. She just fixed it right away.

The following year that first record went on to be one of her biggest of all time. If anything, the joint is even hotter these days. All the pop singers, from Nelly Furtado to Christina Aguilera, are trying on some variation of an R&B/hip-hop crossover, but back then she was the first. Her audience was ready for her to mix it up.

A hit like that usually leads to a remix, so a few months later Mariah had us come to her house to try out a few things. When me, Manuel, and Phil Tan flew up to New York and made the long car ride up to their estate we really didn't know what to expect. Tommy had a scary reputation. There were all these rumors floating around that he was connected to the mob somehow. I didn't know about that stuff, but I did know that everyone was afraid of him. I doubt anyone's ever been whacked, but he had the power to kill careers if somebody was stupid enough to piss him off.

Her place blew my mind. It was the biggest house I'd ever seen, except for the sultan of Brunei's crib. Ralph Lauren's mansion was right up the street, but I bet Tommy and Mariah's place was bigger. The studio was as large as the Hit Factory, and everything in it, all that cutting-edge equipment, was exactly what they had at Sony's studio in Manhattan. The only difference was this one looked out on an Olympic-size indoor pool with a painted blue sky. It was amazing. It was every bit of a house you would want. When I first saw it I said to myself, "Man, I'd love to get me a place like this some day."

Tommy was nice to us despite his scary reputation. We were his guests so he made a point of being the gracious host. We were only there for the day, but he gave us the grand tour. But Mariah only started relaxing when Tommy and his people weren't around. She had household staff, security people, and assistants running around all over the place watching her every move. You couldn't even go to the bathroom without someone coming in right afterward to wipe everything down. It was like they were waiting right outside the door listening when you were doing your do!

We weren't really free to just chill and let the music flow like it would back home in Atlanta. I didn't have all my equipment and toys to work with. It was just me, Phil, Manuel, Mariah, her piano, and about a dozen assistants hovering close by. The expectation was on us to get it done, fast.

The tension got even worse when Brat flew up to record her piece in the remix later that day. In that hushed, uptight environment my lil' sis was like some Tasmanian devil on crack. Tommy had no idea what he signed up for.

When Brat arrived at the mansion she was all nervous. At first she couldn't even write her verse because she was so starstruck over meeting Mariah. MC was just as taken with my lil' sister. Even though Mariah was all girlie with her Hello Kitty obsession and sexy clothes, Brat's tomboy style was like her flip side. Brat acted out the way Mariah wished she could if only she didn't have Tommy's people always watching over her.

Brat couldn't handle how clean and perfect the whole place was. Even the food bothered her. She was hungry, but she didn't want to touch all the fancy caterer stuff like bagels, cut fruit, and cheeses that were laid out in the studio. "This is video shoot food," she said, stamping her feet. Then she did her Brat thing and stirred up some major trouble.

"I'm hungry! Let's go get a cheeseburger," she said to Mariah.

It was the excuse Mariah was looking for to get out of there and go for a joy ride in one of the dozen sports cars she was never allowed to drive. Brat made her feel real bold. Finally Mariah had a partner in crime. She was only too happy to give Brat a ride to McDonald's, so the two of them split without telling anyone where they were going.

People kept asking me, "Where's Mariah, where'd she go?" I didn't know what to tell them. I knew they were probably going out to get some food, but knowing Brat anything could happen.

"Oh shit," I thought. "Tommy's gonna be pissed."

I called Brat. Mariah's cell phone had already rung a dozen times. Brat saw it was me on the caller ID so she picked up. "Yeah J.D., what's goin' on?" she said, all innocent. I could hear Mariah laughing in the background.

"Brat, are you crazy? Where the hell are y'all going?" I said.

"J.D., we're just going to Mickey D's for some burgers, I don't know why everyone keeps calling, it's no big deal," she said.

"Brat, please don't get in the middle of this. Stay outta this shit. Tommy's having a fit. I don't want you to get into any trouble with him. Get back here now!"

"J.D. I'm not the one driving okay," she said. "Mariah's not turning around. We're just going to McDonald's. It's only half a mile up the road!"

The girls weren't gone long, maybe half an hour. But you'd think by everyone's reaction that Mariah was being kidnapped at gunpoint, not getting a cheeseburger and fries. After the incident nothing more was said, but Brat and Mariah have been the best of friends ever since that first lil' joyride together.

Seeing Mariah's life was an awakening for Brat. She was always obsessed with having stuff, ever since that tantrum over the Mickey Mouse watch in the mall. She was just starting to come into her money and thought her platinum album meant she'd be able to buy all that stuff and her life would be happy.

But meeting Mariah, who had all the toys and clothes Brat could ever dream of, and coming to understand how sad and lonely her life was at the time, was just the thing to give Brat some perspective.

Even though she never let it affect her grind as an artist, I'm sure it was tough for Mariah living like some caged canary and being watched all the time. But that's her story to tell in her own book!

Coming off that whole initial success with Mariah I still thought of myself as a hip-hop producer. I never set out to make pop records. I thought the Mariah thing was just some one-off or fluke. But things were taking a whole interesting new direction. Just when I was beginning to wonder if I'd ever find someone I could make into a real star, a skinny 18-year-old kid from Chattanooga was sent my way by none other than L.A. Reid.

Usher Raymond wasn't even signed when we first met a few years earlier, in 1992, when Chris and Chris were hitting it big. Once again, he was a church kid. His mother, Jonetta Patton, had him singing in the choir she led at the Bethel Baptist Church back home. When they moved to Atlanta he couldn't have been more than 13, but he was doing the rounds of all the local talent shows and auditioning for anyone he could.

When I first laid eyes on Usher, I was sitting in a room backstage at the Fox Theater in Atlanta before a Kris Kross performance. Outside that backroom, things were hectic. Little girl fans were running around all over the place, but I was by myself when a local talent scout, A.J. Alexander, brought Usher through to me. He was dressed in his Damaged Wear and he was working his look. I said, "What's up man, how y'all doin'?"

He gave me his squinty smile and asked if I wanted him to sing for me. I knew he wanted me to sign him. But because of Kris Kross, people were bringing kiddie acts to me all the time and he was just one of the many. We exchanged a few polite words but I didn't want to know. He might have had that sparkle but I wasn't looking for it at the time. I didn't want to be dealing with no more kids and their parents!

"Nah, nah, I'm cool," I said. "I just wanted to meet you, man."

Later on, I heard L.A. Reid pulled the trigger and signed him. But nobody knew what to do with the kid. They just kept shuffling him off from one producer to another and I was the last on the list.

First Usher was sent to work with Puffy. At that point Usher was still the quiet choirboy doing talent contests for his stage mother. But Puff was a young man living the single life back then. That was a hard-partying crowd for a teenage boy from Chattanooga to be growing up with.

No telling what he was exposed to. They wanted him to be this bad boy, and Usher thought he had to be that too. But that wasn't who he was. The image didn't work because it wasn't real. That's partly why his first album failed.

I met up with Usher one other time before L.A. finally hooked him up with me to be his main producer. In 1995, we did a session for a remix of "Think of You" and I had him sing the bridge to the song. It was obvious to me even then that they weren't using him right. He had a great voice and star potential.

For a minute he was being sent from one producer to another and nothing was working. Dallas Austin was the last guy to work with Usher before me. Most kids would have lost hope and given up by then, but not Usher. By the age of 11, he already knew music was his path and he firmly believed his career as a singer would happen. He reminded me of me, all determined to move ahead with his career when he was still just a kid. Even as a teenager he had this presence. I don't even know what to call it, except that it was some kinda glow that certain great artists give off.

By the time he came to my house to work on the next album late in '97, it was make or break. He still had the hunger to be a star. He just needed someone who was willing to pay him some attention and give him direction. All along he was waiting for a mentor to help him get to places that he wanted to go. All I ever wanted was someone with true star potential who was willing to trust me and take instruction.

Back then, Usher was a far cry from the sex symbol he became. It was always in him. But that side of him was buried deep. Puberty had been rough on him. He had bad skin until my mom hooked him up with a dermatologist who could take care of his problem. He was spending so much time moped out and not working on himself that he was all skinny.

All he ate was junk food. Usher could inhale a box of Krispy

Kremes in less than an hour. He was living on greasy shit like burgers and fried chicken. When he came over to my house my mom made us Sloppy Joes and he said he'd never had them before. Home cooking was such a treat, he grabbed the last one!

Usher lived far from our house. He was about an hour and a half's drive away in Doraville. It was getting inconvenient, because we were working all night, and I'd have ideas at odd hours of the morning. One time I called Usher at 3 A.M. and said, "Yo man, wake up and get over here."

"Come on, man, you crackin' up, it's the middle of the night!" he said.

"I got this crazy idea and you gotta be here so we can track this real quick," I said.

That night he ended up in a ditch because he was driving so fast along Old National. We decided it was just easier for him to be at the house while we were working on a project. His momma kept close tabs though. She had numbers for every room in our house!

I didn't try to push anything on him. I tried to bring out who Usher really was, not force a particular style or personality on him. To get that done we basically lived together for a spell. He came over to the house, we danced around the living room, had some girls over, talked about music and life, and got to know each other. I would do things like listen in on his phone conversations with girls so I could write his songs the way he really spoke. Usher was still just a teenager at that point, so he was only just getting to know who he was. It was my job to get to know him better than he knew himself.

At the time he didn't realize that was what was going on. Usher just figured we were hanging out. But when we played I had a purpose. He wasn't much into video games, and he didn't want to mess with his money and gamble, but he'd shoot pool with me. We bet push-ups. Every time I lost, which wasn't often, I'd do push-ups. Every time he lost I made him do them.

Usher's real competitive, so those lil' wagers did two things: They built some muscle on him and they motivated him. He got focused on doing everything better. Pretty soon he was all buffed up and his confidence was building. He was a teenager on the cusp of real manhood. Around town he was catching the eyes of some ladies. I could see a theme building.

Usher was always trippin' on some girl. Good or bad, he was always in a relationship when it came time to do an album. They were usually a little older than him and sometimes on the shady side. I first noticed it when we started work on the *My Way* album. We had a conversation about some girl he was with at the time. From what he was saying I could tell she was looking for different things in life but he didn't believe me. He was convinced she'd stay with him no matter what, and that no one could take her away from him. But he was way too young to be thinking that way.

"This girl is gonna break your heart," I warned him.

"Nah," he said. "My girl's never gonna go nowhere."

A few months later, on New Year's Eve, we went out to a

club called Atlanta Live. The girl wanted to dance but Usher wasn't into it. Usher went off to the bathroom and she must've figured it was okay to dance with some other dude, and that's the first thing Usher saw when he came back. I guess all those things I was telling him over the past few months, about giving a girl too much credit, were rushing through his mind, because when he saw what she was doing he was mad. They had a huge argument in the middle of the dance floor. What that girl was doing might have been innocent, but Usher stormed out of there, jumped into the limo, and left her in the club.

In spite of all the drama with women, Usher somehow makes it all come together in the studio. At the end of the day he has the self-discipline to channel all those emotions into a great song. Of all the artists I've ever worked with he's the best at taking heed of what you say. He's willing to learn and grow with you but still be his own man. We were both comfortable around each other from the get-go and that vibe we had together made it easy for me to write for him. Whatever it is he's going through at the time, he lets it come out in the music and other people can really feel him. Our first album together, My Way, sold seven million units. It was all about Usher taking control.

Usher found his own voice with his first hit single, "U Make Me Wanna." He was the sex symbol who was the nice guy at heart. When he performed he'd show off his six-pack and wink at the women. He did this thing where he'd pick girls out from the audience, but never know which one to take home. It was working for him, at least in terms of sales, but he wasn't even

20. People loved him but I knew he could do better. He needed more of the kind of depth that experience brings. Usher was still a work in progress.

It was another three years before we hooked up again on Usher's second album, *8701*. By then he was really living the lifestyle. When he was 13 and first auditioned for L.A. at his house in Alpharetta, after announcing that he was going to be his next star Usher said, "This is going to be mine someday." He bought the house. He had all the fast cars and jewelry. He was dating models, actresses, and singers and playing the field. But he'd still get himself messed up over women.

Usher loves real hard. I've seen him in the studio where he's so into a girl he can't even record. One time a girl kept calling him when he was in the vocal booth and he couldn't stay focused. He was just jittering. He'd sing a few lines and leave. He was moving around so much I could tell the girl was messing with him. He mentioned something about it to me and my co-producer, Bryan Michael Cox, and as he was leaving I said, "You got it bad." After that me and Bryan just looked at each other. By the time Usher came back I had written the hook and first verse.

"You Got it Bad," was our next hit single. I wrote most of it while Usher was torturing himself. Like always, whatever Usher was going through came out in his song.

He trusted me enough to let that happen. Years later he told me he came to think of me as his brother by the way I handled a situation with some other shady woman he was caught up with.

I had a bad feeling about her when Usher told me his girl told him she dreamt she had sex with me in the studio.

The fact that she had this dream, and decided to tell her man about it, seemed off to me. I've dealt with a lot of females in this business and some of them are worse playas than the men. I told Usher it didn't sound right and he wasn't to bring her back to SouthSide any more. With all these guys hanging out in here it would be just my luck that she'd be here waiting on Usher and get herself caught flirting with some other man. It was very possible that if she was dreaming about straying that it was on her mind. I couldn't risk this girl doing something stupid and ruining my relationship with Usher.

Usher was getting to be more like a man and less like a lost baby boy by the time we hooked up on our last album, *Confessions*. As far as our experiences with women and life were concerned, we were more or less equal by then, so when we talked I wasn't just some big brother giving advice to a young buck. We had real, deep conversations about life. And Usher does love to talk about life!

This time he was really in love, not just play play. He hooked up with Chilli from TLC, a woman of similar standing in the music industry who had her own money. It wasn't the case of a beautiful gold digger preying on the innocent. But as usual with Usher, it was intense. There was so much jealousy and strife toward the end of that relationship he was actually in pain.

One night he had a deep conversation with a lady friend about it.

"Man, I just don't want to go through that feeling when you're in a relationship, it just hurts too much," he told her.

"You've just got to let it burn, even if it burns right out," she said to him. "Just let it go and go with it."

Immediately, he needed to escape into the music and work it out. So right after that discussion, at 2 A.M., he ran back to my studio and said, "J.D., I got an idea man. We should write a song called 'Let It Burn.'"

"Huh? What's that mean?" I asked.

"You know that feeling when you're going through it and you just gotta let it go," he said. "I don't know any other way to describe it except that it's a burning feeling."

I said, "Okay, cool," and started writing.

We had our first big single off the album. "Burn" was a hit because it was also everybody's song—something we've all been through. It was 2004 by the time we got together on that record. Things in my life were straight. By then I'd found my soul mate, Janet. But I had plenty of my own shit from the past to draw from when we were writing those songs.

That monthlong break I took from Tiffany, a few years before, turned into something you just couldn't go back from. I was out at the Atlanta Live club one night when I met up with a girl from the neighborhood named Pamela Sweat and got her number. I don't remember this myself, but Pam told me we'd met before when I flagged her down on Old National. I guess I had my eye on her before we reunited in the club. I don't know what it was about her, but I just couldn't resist.

From that point on we spent every day and every night together. Pam was always over at my house. We became real tight and for a minute I forgot all about Tiffany. I think I might have even been in love. Then one night I got a call from Pam with some big news.

"J.D., I'm pregnant and you're the father," she said.

Now, ahead of her making that phone call someone had been telling her that if a man says "What?!" in response to a statement like that it means he's gonna ask the woman to have an abortion. That's not what I was thinking. In fact, the idea of having a kid was kind of exciting to me. But at the time I guess the question of what I was going to tell Tiffany, who was still my unofficial/official girlfriend, was going through my mind. So I walked straight into it and said, "What?!"

It was a typical response from a guy who's dealing with two women. It was a normal reaction to a surprise like that, period. My whole life I kept it strapped up. My mom had me when she was still in her teens, so she was always on me to be careful and make sure I didn't go and get a girl pregnant before I had my career all straight. Until then, I'd pretty much followed her advice, but I was 25 years old and my career was going fine. Having a kid with Pam, someone I felt really close to, didn't seem so bad. It's just that the circumstances were kinda messy.

But Pam automatically went on the defensive. Before I even had a second to let the news sink in she said, "Well you won't have to worry about the kid. I'll get back together with my ex-boyfriend and raise the child with him."

Now, back in those days, when I was a younger J.D. with a lot of money, you couldn't tell me something stupid like that because I took it literally. I thought to myself, "Okay well fuck it then." I told Pam, "You and your boyfriend deal with it then, I'll talk to you later."

Anger, cockiness, and the Virgo in me made me not speak to Pam for a whole nine months and then some. My feelings were hurt. I got it in my mind that if I didn't talk to her, maybe it wasn't really happening. It was like we were playing chess. She was trying to get the upper hand and I was calling her bluff. I didn't want to not have a baby, but if someone pisses me off, I have no problem cutting them out of my life and never speaking to them again. I've done it a few times. I'll walk away and never look back and people don't even know what hit them. I didn't realize there are some things you just can't walk away from.

I immediately got back together with Tiffany and tried to put that whole chapter with Pam behind me. There was hell to pay with Tiffany, but I talked my way out of it. Of course, it never felt right and I was still very much into Pam. It's always hard to go back to the way things used to be. There were plenty of rumors floating around town that I got a girl pregnant, but she took me back for a spell.

All that became the subject of a conversation me and Usher were having a few years later, when we were in the studio writing his last album. That's even how the name of the album came up. We always start with a name, so Usher said, "Let's make an album about real situations and call it *Real Talk*." Instead, we called it *Confessions*.

At the time, it seemed like everyone was having baby mama and relationship issues. We were all talking about what happens when you cheat on your main girl and get caught red-handed. Not that I cheated. When you're on a break from your girl you're on a break and other women are fair game. But I never told Tiffany about Pam after we got back together. Until I had to.

The first record, "Confessions Pt. I," was about a guy who used to lie to his girlfriend all the time. He was always going out of town and saying it was for work when he was really doing something else with an old flame who lived in a different city. That was the joint that got everyone in the media talking about Usher as the badass ladykiller who was cheating on Chilli.

It wasn't strictly-speaking autobiographical, but it was just true enough to create the kind of media story and buzz that L.A. Reid wanted on his star's album. People were feeling Usher's persona was a tad too bland and genial. Me, Usher, and L.A. wanted something that would give Usher an edge.

Our conversations turn into the greatest records. But what people don't realize is that "Confessions Pt. II" is really my story with Usher's own sexed-up lil' spin. It wasn't my intention to put it out there, but "Part I," Usher's story, just naturally ended where my real-life situation began, with me cheating on my steady girl-friend, having a baby with another woman, and having to confess everything that happened when it was time to face my main girl.

The story came spilling out. I knew it would be huge because when I make hits, they come quick like that. In 2004, *Confessions* the album won 11 *Billboard* awards and took home three Grammys. Not that I personally took home a Grammy. I lost in my category to the Ray Charles album. I guess it wasn't my time yet.

# 11

# LOVE ON MY MIND

When my baby girl Shaniah was born, in 1998, I was scared. I lived my whole life putting work before everything else. I always figured no one, not even a girlfriend I thought I was in love with, could ever be more important to me than my music. Until I became a father.

Throughout that whole time Pam was pregnant with my daughter and a few months after, I was living in deep denial. This all happened during the height of my balling out-of-control phase when I was living and spending in the fast lane. I wasn't in the mood for playing around. I thought Pam wasn't taking me seriously for who I was and I was gonna show her. I drank and partied a lot, so it was easy for me to push serious stuff out of my mind. I kept myself in a protective bubble with liquor and work.

Somehow I also believed it would actually be possible to let another man raise my child and not worry about it. That might have been the case with regular people, but not a rich guy in the music business like me. Someone in my position has to take care of his child and his baby mama. It's a point of honor that you set them up in a house, pay the bills, and give the mother of your child a monthly check so she can stay home and look after your baby. You've got the money so there's no excuse. In this industry, if you don't look after your baby AND your baby mama, you're an asshole. It's a code that makes guys like me a target.

But that's not even where my head was at when Shaniah was born. I guess I was burying the pain and shock of what was happening. Even though I was determined to stay on my hiatus, the truth never went away entirely. People around College Park would come up to me and say, "Yo J.D., I hear you got a child." I'd just say, "Yeah, whateva."

But subconsciously I kinda knew it was really happening. I was having symptoms: weird dreams, cravings, weight gain. I was experiencing all that sympathy a man goes through when his woman is having a baby.

Then one day, when Shaniah was about six months old, I was sitting alone relaxing in my swimming pool when some papers landed in our mailbox. It was Shaniah's birth certificate, hand-delivered and not even put inside an envelope. Whoever did that, probably Pam, knew what they were doing, because my mom always picks up the mail and she was sure to be the first one to see it.

"Jermaine, is there something you've been hiding from me?" she asked.

"No, what do you mean?" I said.

"Well, this paper here says you have a daughter and her name is Shaniah," she said, reading out the date, time, place of birth, the baby's weight, and so on.

She handed me the paper and I went numb. I sat there in the pool, stone-faced and unable to move for the rest of the night. It finally hit me that this was real. I thought, "Wow, I have a child!" I knew it was time for me to man up and be a father.

There was just one problem: Tiffany. We'd been back together for close to a year. But I had no choice. Shaniah was born and she was going to be a part of my life so I had to finally tell my girlfriend that I had a child with another woman. I knew that chapter with Tiffany would be over.

I got in touch with Pam. As soon as the reality of the situation sunk in, I was desperate to see my new baby girl. I wasn't sure what to do at first. I always had plenty of pets but I never had any contact with little babies before. I was nervous I might drop her. Then, after less than a minute of holding her, this feeling, almost like a chemical reaction, kicked in.

All those feelings of love and protectiveness just welled up inside me and I became a daddy. My throat went all tight and my eyes welled up. Even now, nine years later, I just can't believe that I had something to do with creating this little girl. It's almost surreal.

Of course, it wasn't long before my lil' girl inspired a poem:

*Something so beautiful*
*I never thought I could create,*
*You've brought new life,*
*Into my lonely heart*
*And you ain't never got to worry,*
*'bout us being apart.*
*The joy you bring to me*
*You'll never know,*
*And there's nothing more*
*Exciting, than watching you grow*
*Into a beautiful, intelligent*
*Black woman.*
*Look out world!*

Before Shaniah, I never believed I had time for anything personal. I've never been one for just being still or hanging out and doing nothing without a purpose that's work-related. But she made my world bigger somehow. I got a whole new perspective on life and the importance of making time for family.

I actually got back together with Pam and we stayed a couple for about three years. It was easy with her because we were friends. We never actually lived together full-time under the same roof, but we were a family, and of all the women I'd been with up until that point Pam was the one I got along with best. Even when we finally split, we were able to stay on good terms and come together over the welfare of our child. When it comes to Shaniah, me and Pam are somewhat on the same page.

I can't be the parent 24/7. If I did that I wouldn't be able to be the provider. But I call my daughter all the time and see her every chance I get. My mom brings her over to the studio, even when it's way past her bedtime. When I'm not traveling all over the place, the weekends are when we have our time together. We do whatever Shaniah wants to do, whether it's playing in the pool, running around in the yard with my other kids—my bulldogs Slash, Ya Ya, and Rocky—or shopping at Toys "R" Us.

I couldn't even tell you who she takes after. She's pretty, like her mother, but everyone says she's all feisty, just like her grandma Tina. And other people say we look just like each other.

I reckon she's growing up to be a workaholic like me. When my mom takes her over to her place, Shaniah goes with her to meetings and brings along her own little briefcase. My daughter can't stand the idea of just sitting around doing nothing. First thing out of her mouth when she gets up in the morning is, "What are we doing today?"

I keep a set of Barbie dolls at the studio. But she's either in the middle of the conversations around the kitchen, hanging out inside one of the office cubicles pretending to answer the phone, or bugging Tad and Rufus, my production assistants.

From the beginning, I always thought of myself as a parent to the younger artists I hooked up with, but real fatherhood is so much larger. Even Bow Wow, the closest thing to a son I've ever had, doesn't get under my skin the way Shaniah does. She taught me how to make time for someone and love unconditionally. I guess you could say she prepared me so that when I finally met my soul mate, I was ready.

# 12

# WE BELONG TOGETHER

**M**e and Jan were acquaintances, then friends, for a long time before we finally got together. I doubt she even remembers the first time we ever rubbed shoulders 17 years ago. It was 1990 and she was on her *Rhythm Nation* tour. She was still married and had a lot going on in her life at the time. I was with Kris Kross and we happened to be backstage at her show.

Growing up I always had a crush on Janet. Every guy from my generation was more or less crazy about her, from the time she showed up on those TV shows like *Good Times* and *Diff'rent Strokes* and later in those videos for her *Control* album. I know it sounds corny, but she has that kind of smile you just want to see all the time.

For that first meeting, I decided I was gonna to play it all cool. I tried on the swagger and said, "Hey, what's up? How y'all doin'?" Then when it was time to say good-bye I kinda flew a flirt at her and said, "I'll see you again." I don't think she even paid me any attention.

It was all about Kris Kross back then anyway. Those were my young, fly, and flashy days and I was deep into myself, my work, and all those things money could buy. You get so caught up in your own shit, and so locked up in your own lil' fortress, that when you do see people outside of your world you don't really see them. Back then I wasn't ready for that big, life-changing love.

Janet was probably more or less aware of who I was professionally. We continued to cross paths in small ways. One time Brat was hanging out with her and some other people at the Viper Room on Sunset in Hollywood. She was celebrating their win at the Source Awards with Busta Rhymes and they hooked up with Janet at the after party.

Brat knew all about my infatuation so she called me up and said, "Yo, J.D., get down here! Your girl Janet is with us at the club!"

I rushed over. I don't think we even spoke other than to just say "hey." Once again, Janet didn't pay me any attention. She was married at the time, and anyway I was really just supposed to be there for Brat. It was enough for me to get a chance to look at my crush in person.

Everyone says it's ironic that I ended up doing a remix of Janet's "Someone to Call My Lover." They just assume that's how we got together. But when the executives at her label at the time, Virgin, asked me to do it, me and Janet weren't even friends.

That soon changed. Jan's real hands-on when it comes to her music. Someone at Virgin gave her my number so she could speak to me directly about what she wanted on her remix. It was the first time she actually called my phone. We had a nice, professional conversation. I asked her what she wanted from the remix. Maybe I tried to linger on the phone a little. I figured it would be the last time she ever called me, but she gave me her pager number so I knew how to get in touch.

After the remix came out we stayed in contact. Every now and then I'd send her a message just to keep the conversation going and be friends. But Janet had a friend named Julie who was my stylist and became the real "in" to the object of my affection.

Whenever Julie was working with me I'd tell her to send Janet a message. I'd make little jokes and Julie used to call Janet with me making my witty remarks in the background. It was easy for us to click in a casual way. I was somebody in the business Jan could laugh and relax with, no pressure. We were both kids who grew up in the industry, so we could relate to each other on a certain level. But Julie was the glue in between me and Janet. Our mutual friend was putting our relationship together and helping me turn a friendship into something more.

It was Julie who told me Jan wanted a silver Timeport Skytel pager for her thirty-fifth birthday. I had the hookup with Motorola so I had first dibs on every lil' hot piece of technology that was coming out. I immediately got my hands on one to give it to her.

Janet told me later she thought I was trying to be all slick about the situation when I gave her a two-way pager for a birthday present. She likes to joke with people that I gave it to her because I knew that she'd automatically feel obligated to exchange contact information with me. But it was flat-out a gift! I already had her number!

From that point, we did start paging each other on a more regular basis. I started off by trying to make her laugh, which wasn't hard. Then I gradually got deeper and let her know my innermost thoughts. She didn't always page me back. Sometime afterward she told me I made her jaw drop, but for a minute I thought I might've scared her off. She was at a point in her life when she just figured she was done with men, so when I said stuff that was too close to the heart she closed up at first.

Then she started answering me back. Next thing I knew we were paging each other constantly, like many times an hour. No matter where we were in the world, we'd be going back and forth with our thoughts. We still weren't lovers. Our minds got together before our bodies did.

We're alike, me and Jan. People assume we're out there and all extroverted because we get up onstage and perform. It's easy when you have a job to do and you have to be a certain way in front of a crowd. You play a role because it has a purpose. But outside of that performance mode we can both be introverts. One-on-one I'm not too quick to let people in either. I only trust a few people, and even they don't get to see that inner core, that lil' nugget of who I am underneath all the layers. Janet's like that too.

So many years of being in this business and dealing with people who betray you or put shit out there that isn't true makes you cautious. Janet's the sweetest, most fun person I know, but if she doesn't know you she takes a minute to warm up. She's all self-protective and quiet until someone really earns her trust. That's why when you do get that 1,000-watt smile from her it lights up your world. It's like you won a prize or something.

I don't even know how I got so much work done that year, we were messaging each other so much. It was getting spooky how inside each other's heads we were. I'd be just about to page her about something, and she'd message me before I hit the send button saying exactly what I was going to say. I'll keep the contents to myself. Let's just say it was like we really were reading each other's minds!

In 2001, I had a lot on my plate. Besides my So So Def artists I was busy handling dozens of side projects. Right before the terrorist attacks of September 11, 2001 happened, U2's Bono asked me to produce a record to raise awareness and money for AIDS in Africa. We called it, *What's Going On*, and the record had Bono, Destiny's Child, Jennifer Lopez, *NSYNC, Nelly, Ja Rule, the Backstreet Boys, Britney Spears, Alicia Keys, basically everyone who was hot at the time. After the World Trade Center was attacked some people in the media were giving us a bad rap saying hip-hop ballers like me didn't care about what was happening in the world, but I was in New York finishing up work on the AIDS record on September 9, just two days before it all went down.

For about three days, my engineers Phil Tan and Johnny Horesco didn't even sleep. There were rainstorms so we waited all night to catch our flight to New York and got there to find out everyone else's flights had been delayed too. By the time they were all there we had about half an hour each to get all the artists' vocals recorded. There were long, tedious sessions of editing so many different versions of the song, cutting vocals, and splicing together different artists. Then we had to run around, do interviews, you name it. But by the time the two towers were hit, I was already in Los Angeles.

Appropriately enough, Bono decided to turn the project into something for the victims of the World Trade Center and put the news footage of what happened into the video. Right after that my dad launched Hip Hop 4 Humanity to help raise money for the United Way's September 11 Fund, kids with AIDS in Africa, and the victims of hurricane Katrina. Hip Hop 4 Humanity is my dad's thing, not mine. But I try to do my part to help out.

A few months later in April 2002, another more personal tragedy hit. My girl Lisa "Left Eye" Lopes from TLC was killed in a car crash in Honduras. Me and Jan went to the service at the New Birth Mission Baptist Church on May 3 together. There were thousands of people at that funeral. It was a sad time, but I had Janet by my side. The two of us walked into the church hand in hand. Everyone thought we were together at that point, but we were still just friends.

Two weeks later, on May 16, I threw Jan a big birthday bash in Miami. By then our friendship had moved ahead. In my mind, we were a couple, although Jan told me we were only "seeing each other" at that point. I still wasn't allowed to think of myself as her man. She'd just come off a bad marriage and wasn't about to go jumping into something heavy just yet.

But I hung in there. I wasn't about to let a girl like that get away. Then, in September, Janet gave me the best birthday present of my life. She paged me asking me what I was doing to celebrate. I said I didn't have any special plans, so she invited me to go to some exclusive Caribbean island I'd never heard of. Immediately I said, "Hell yeah!"

That was the first real vacation I ever went on in my life. All the other trips I ever made, even those weekends in Miami or Vegas, were about the business. Before Janet, I'd never even taken a day to just do nothing. I didn't understand how it was possible. But that island was special. You have to have money to go there. You can only get to it by private plane. It's a sophisticated, world-class pleasure island in the West Indies. Tommy Hilfiger and David Bowie had houses there, but it's so quiet and exclusive you never see them.

I'm not gonna tell you the name of the island where we went. I'm so afraid if word gets out then everyone else in the music business will try to go there and take it over like they have in Anguilla. I want to protect it as one of the few places where me and Jan can go to really be alone.

For two whole weeks there was no one around, no one wanting a piece of me, no way anyone could reach me on my pager.

I'm not the type to open up with anyone, but me and Jan talked for hours by the pool. We were so in sync it was like we could see right into each other's souls. We still have these deep conversations all the time. I call Jan my therapist.

Where we stayed was the most beautiful place I'd ever seen. It was so exclusive I felt like I had it all to myself. I looked around me as if I was really seeing people, places, and things for the first time in my life. I was like a blind man who gets his sight back and suddenly sees the hills, the trees, the sea, and the sky in Technicolor. It was just me, the beach, and Janet. It was the perfect place to fall in love. By the time we got back I was head over heels. We've been an item ever since.

Things have always been so easy between us. There was none of the usual pressure I felt with my girlfriends in the past. Like me, my girl was deep in the business from day one. Like me, her family was always involved. Like me, she was constantly traveling and working. She understands how your work can take you away. She does get jealous, but with her I'm not always on the defensive, trying to explain how it is.

It wasn't long after we got together on that dream vacation when I met her whole family. It was Thanksgiving weekend when they invited me down to L.A. for a gathering. They don't do Thanksgiving, but they get together for a big family dinner.

I was real nervous. When it's a girl with six brothers of course you're gonna be intimidated. I was thinking the worst and worried they would ask me all the hard questions of life. I knew they'd be real protective of the baby in the family. But

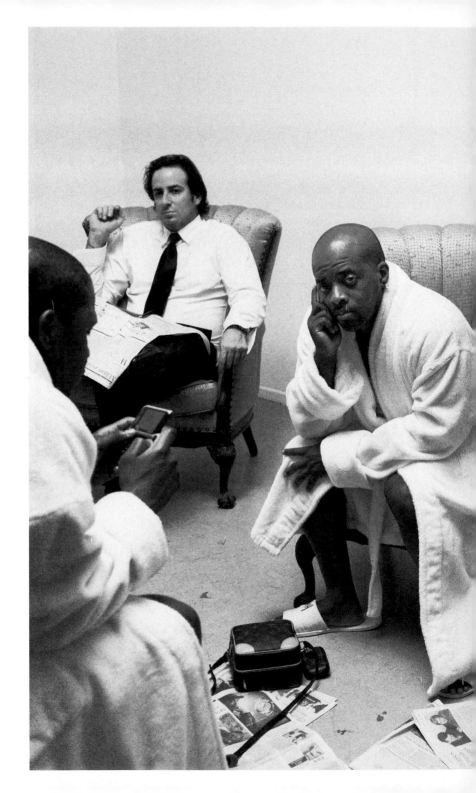

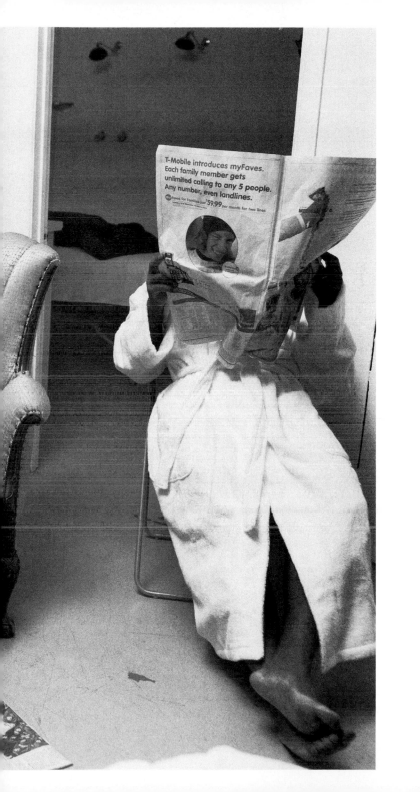

they didn't grill me at all. They were just real gracious and nice, joking around with each other and saying, "Pass the biscuits please."

I couldn't get over how normal the whole family was. The Jacksons were just a regular black family with black people shit going on! They play board games together. Jan's mom is even more competitive than I am. She can't stand to lose and she won't give it up to anyone. The kids all argue and tease each other like siblings do and throw down when it's time to eat. They tease me too. La Toya's always making fun of me and mimicking me on the phone. Jan finds it hilarious.

The Jacksons let me in with open arms. When they were all going through it over Michael's trial, I spoke up for them. I wanted to defend the family's honor. They're just nice, loving people who deserved better than getting raked over the coals in the media. I also did it because it was important for Janet. The trial was rough on her. She and Michael were always so close.

Getting together with Jan was the first time in my life I felt like I was with a woman who's also a friend and a partner. I feel like I can breathe around her. Now I have someone who is more than my equal and who I can bounce things off of. Jan will give me an intelligent answer. She's educated and she knows stuff.

Life with Jan is just real normal. When we hang out, we hang out at home. She's a homebody. We don't want to be out on the road all the time.

Aside from the house I bought for me and my mother in College Park I had a couple of condos around town. Just before Shaniah was born I moved out of Dix-Lee-On, and divided my time at different spots depending on what I was doing and which part of town I was working or partying at. SouthSide, which I built six years ago, even has a couple of bedroom suites for those late night sessions. One of them is my assistant Tyrone's crib.

But after buying and selling several condos and houses, I finally found my dream place in an exclusive part of Buckhead. It's got enough light for my birds, enough yard for my dogs to run around, and enough space inside to entertain women as sophisticated as Janet is. She helped me decorate, a lil'. She even started calling it her house. It's MY crib, but I'm glad she feels at home!

People might be surprised by my taste. The place looks like it's straight out of *House & Garden*. I've got a few valuable paintings. Janet's the one who got me interested in collecting art. When I first came to her apartment in New York the first things I noticed were a Matisse and a Picasso hanging on her walls. I loved them! I'm into that era, but my favorites are Warhol and Lichtenstein. I was always into Pop Art. I have an eye for beautiful things in general. But Janet has a way of getting me to tap into a passion that's already there and take it further. She doesn't impose her taste on me. She just helps me refine what's already mine.

For now Jan's official home is in L.A., but she hangs out

with me in Buckhead whenever I'm home and she's not traveling. We drive around the city and watch people. We get takeout. We buy strawberry smoothies from Smoothie King. We
watch our shows, *The Sopranos* and *Entourage.* If Jan's around
on weekends and holidays we hang out with my daughter,
Shaniah.

I couldn't understand that whole rumor about Jan being
pregnant, or having a child in secret. That crazy gossip just
won't go away. If Jan were to have a child, neither of us would
want to keep it a secret. We're both in a place in our lives where
we'd be happy to have a kid together. I could do the Jacksons all
over again and have a whole crew. We already operate like a
family as it is.

Life as a couple ain't always perfect. We have our lil' beefs.
Hah! At first, we argued about who'd pay. I'm the man so I like
to be the one who's doing the providing, but in the past she
always took care of things for the men in her life. I couldn't understand how a man could let a beautiful woman like that shell
out all the time, no matter how successful she was. It made no
sense to me. But she was used to it. She wasn't comfortable
with me paying. We finally worked it out where we take turns
treating each other.

Janet also gets on my case sometimes. I was an only child,
so I always had my mom to pick up after me. And, as I said
before, I like things messy. Whatever I take off stays right where
it is. You can always tell when I'm home because my stuff is
there, mostly on the floor.

It drives Janet crazy. She grew up in a strict house full of kids who had to do their chores. They had to wash clothes, vacuum, everything. Every Saturday they all had to pitch in and clean the whole yard. She's always telling me to tidy up. Since I've been with her I do try to clean up once in a while. The first time I ever made a bed was after we started dating. I don't do it all the time, but every so often.

It's well worth any extra little effort. To be able to have a real conversation about different things in life puts me on a whole new level. You always need someone to mellow you out in life. You never know if you're thinking right or wrong until you take a step. It's like some big chess game. If you make the wrong move you might lose, so you need a partner you can respect to help you think it through or have your back when you're up against it.

Of course, other people don't see it that way. They just care about whether or not you look good together. People were buggin' out because I wasn't some pretty boy. It just goes to show you how shallow people are. As soon as word got out we were a pair it started some weird mini-controversy. Like people couldn't imagine Jan being with anyone but some movie star. Everyone was saying, "How'd he get a girl like that?" People thought it was some sort of joke. Until I hooked up with Janet I wasn't in the spotlight that much and I couldn't figure out how folks could be so nasty.

It was the same when people were making a big deal about Jan putting on a few pounds. Members of the press were always coming up to me to ask the dumbest questions, like, "So how do you feel about Janet's weight gain?"

"I love Janet whatever size she is," I told one magazine writer. "As a partner you're supposed to understand what somebody's going through."

For real? Do I really need to tell people that? She's my woman! It just meant that, for a minute, there was more of her to love. It proves how superficial the media can be that they would zero in on something so trivial. I don't get how people can even think that way.

It's one thing for people to talk smack about me. It's not my problem if they're too shallow to see what's inside. Say what you want. I know what the truth is. It says more about them than it does about the real situation, so I get over it. But I get more upset when they start attacking my girl.

I stepped down from the Atlanta chapter of the Recording Academy when they uninvited her to the 2004 Grammys after the Super Bowl thing. Somebody in the street said, "Jermaine, that's your girl! How you gonna be president of a chapter in the same organization that actually called your woman and said they don't want her to be a part of their show?" I needed to clean my hands of it.

That whole thing was an early taste of what it's like to be president of something in name only. I didn't understand the point of having a title like that if I couldn't have any influence or power over a decision that was so clearly wrong. It was the members of the Los Angeles chapter who were doing the deciding. It was frustrating, and I couldn't do anything about it. It wouldn't be the first time I'd find out that being president doesn't mean shit when you're not really in charge.

As for that whole incident, I didn't even see the wardrobe mishap go down myself. I was on the playing field, watching the monitor, and I just looked away for a second at what was going on in the crowd when it happened. The whole thing just kinda blew past me at the time. When I went backstage everyone seemed fine with the show. Jan was exhausted from a week's worth of tough rehearsals. But as far as I could tell it was all cool and regular, just like any other artist's gig.

I wasn't that involved in Jan's career at the time, so it's not like I was there in the dressing room with her. I would always just stand outside and wait until the post-performance routine was over. They were probably having a conversation about it that I wasn't aware of.

That pretty much sums up where I stood in terms of Jan's career until I worked on her album as president of Virgin. I was outside the door. As the boyfriend it wasn't my role to be that closely involved in her life as a performer.

Of course, at the time, I knew something was up because it wasn't long before my pager started to blow up with everyone asking me about what happened. I didn't hit anyone back. It was what it was, an accident, and there was nothing to answer or explain.

I could go on for pages about how it was unfair and crazy the way things went down in the aftermath, with all the politics and money involved. I was upset by the way people were treating my girl. But y'all know this already, because the media hasn't grown tired of talking about this subject for more than three years. And now I've said all I'm gonna say. It's ancient history. If there's any more of this story to tell, you'll just have to wait for Janet to write her own book!

# 13

# BEWARE OF DOG

It wasn't long after Shaniah was born when I started feeling dissatisfied with the way things were over at Sony/Columbia. Something about having a kid makes you want to do a better job of handling your business. Even though I was bringing them so many hits, I started feeling like I just wasn't being valued and I wanted more of a say in how things went down.

It started with me making my first album as a performer. I always said I didn't want to be the guy out front, but by then I was a featured artist on so many other artists' albums that it sorta made sense to try it on my own. Besides, I had people like L.A. Reid constantly in my ear about doing my own record. L.A. was convinced it was something the kids wanted to see. I wasn't so sure, but then one day he took me to dinner at one of his favorite restaurants in Atlanta, Mumbo Jumbo.

"J.D., you gotta do this. I love watching you do your thing. You know you can rap, you know you can perform. Why not give it a shot?" he said.

I wasn't being receptive to the idea. I didn't have a problem with rapping on my artists' records or doing cameos in their videos. I never shied away from the limelight. But something told me to let people see me through my artists.

L.A. was always on me to do something as an artist in my own right. After all those glimpses of me on other records he wanted to see and hear more. He wasn't trying to sign me, he was just being a fan. He said he'd be happy just to coproduce something even if it wasn't on his label. But I wasn't 100 percent into it. I didn't think it was my role to take center stage and be a star. I was fighting it. Either that or it was just the cocky side of me just trying to hear enough people say go and do it!

Maybe enough people did get in my ear because later I started thinking it might be fun to rap about my lifestyle and show everyone how I live through my rhymes. I've always believed in stepping back and letting the artists I work with shine, but it was just possible I did have something to say that could stand on its own. It could be a way of branding myself in a way that was separate from producing. Maybe I could pump up the value of my stock. I could also promote my favorite artists by having them do feature spots. If it was a hit it would only benefit Columbia. Seemed worth a shot.

I called the album *Life in 1472*. The theme was all about the Life of J.D. J is the 10th letter of the alphabet and D is the fourth, and I was born in '72, hence the title. I wanted this album to give people an idea of what would've happened if Richie Rich were a rapper. Instead of the beefin' raps that were going on at the time, my rhymes were to be all about the lifestyle, with the cars, the diamonds, and the girls.

The whole album was as much about showcasing the who's who of R&B and hip-hop artists of the day: Usher, Jay-Z, Mariah, Lil' Kim, DMX, Mase, Slick Rick, Snoop, Young Bloodz, Keith Sweat, Brat, Nas, everyone, as it was about me. But I loved it when we went to Spain to make the video for "Sweetheart," featuring Mariah Carey. Having Mariah, one of the hottest stars in the music business, sing my hook was a thrill. Hype Williams, the director, made me dance right on top of the Guggenheim Museum in Bilbao. It made me feel like I was king, looking down on all the R&B and pop charts I was killin'!

The first single we made was "Money Ain't a Thang," a record I made with Jay-Z. He was a highly respected name in rap back then, but nowhere near as big as he is now. Those were his "Can't Knock the Hustle" days. You could really feel his come up.

Before we even met he was doing mixtapes when I did the remix for Dru Hill's song "In My Bed" with Brat. That was one of the first records where New Yorkers were really loving what I did. I finally broke down New York radio because the DJs were all over my production. I even got a Hot 97 remix award for it that year.

In his own way, Jay paid me tribute by taking and freestyling one of my lines, "Y'all wanna dance, I wanna make ya dance." He was using that same phrasing on his records. I was kinda shocked that he even noticed what I was doing, but I thought to myself, "Okay, he's diggin' what I'm doing. That's a good sign."

So when we met for the first time in 1997 on a Biggie tribute video shoot, "We'll Always Love Big Poppa," I remembered what he did. When we were introduced I said, "Oh I heard y'all took my little line!"

"Yeah, I did!" he said. "Let's hook up one time and mess around."

From that point on we were cool. He flew down to Atlanta to give me a verse on a Toni Braxton remix I was working on. Over the next few months we kinda got into a relationship where we'd talk on the phone. When I was ready to do my album he was one of the first ones on the plane to come to my studio.

I did the same thing he did to me and played with a line from one of his records.

It sounded exactly like what I was doing in Atlanta back then. By the time Jay-Z got to my place I already had the hook. Then he added his part, I added my part, and we kept going back and forth until we had it. The whole thing took less than two hours. That's how I knew it would be a hit. To this day it's on my top five list of favorite songs.

That joint went all the way to the top. In fact, the whole album went multiplatinum. It felt good to get the recognition and be the one up front. I didn't even mind all the comparisons to Puffy. People kept saying I was trying to be like him. Well, they had to say something.

I was 25 years old and enjoying a nice big bump to my profile. I never did much in the way of interviews before then. I was so high on the success, it was enough for me to know that I was doing my shit before anyone else was really on the scene.

But you can't be in the spotlight without catching some criticism. I got myself typecast with that "Money Ain't a Thang" joint and all the rest of the high-life music on the album. Other rappers say they see killing in the projects, but I never did. Why should I say I'm a thug if I'm not? My life is what it is. I'm content with being who I am.

I don't write shit down if it's fake. If you hear me say I've got 10 cars, I've got 10 cars. If I say I've got a big-ass house, I've got a big-ass house. On that album I was a rapper who was letting everybody know I had 10 years in the game and I was rich. I was driving Bentleys and Porsches every day. Why would I tell people I was taking the train?

To some extent I was playing my baller role to its hilt for the entertainment value, but of course people can't understand that. Bitchy newspaper headlines said things like, JERMAINE DUPRI PUTS ALL HIS EGO IN ONE BASKET, or YOUNG, RICH & NUMB.

When you put stuff out there people just think that's all you are. They don't know or care about any of the stuff you do behind the scenes, like buying toys for poor kids at Christmas or paying for housing for Katrina victims. Why should they? If you feel it in your heart you do something about it then shut up.

The extra heat was just the price of fame. I think it made me better at understanding all the crazy stuff an artist goes through once they start getting a shine on. As far as the artists in my life were concerned, it made me a better parent!

And just in time too. By 2000, I delivered Columbia their next big star: Lil' Bow Wow. Snoop discovered Shad Moss when he was just six years old. Snoop was doing a stop at Columbus, Ohio, near Bow's home, on his Chronic Tour. In a crowd of about 20,000 people, Snoop spotted Bow, pointed his finger at him and said, "Bring little man up here!"

Bow was real comfortable up on stage, and did what he did naturally when he was home, kinda like a younger version of me when I danced for Diana Ross. From that point on Snoop named him Lil' Bow Wow and took him on the rest of the tour with him.

But it took a minute before I met the kid. First time was way back in 1998 when he was only 11. Snoop and my buddy Steve Prudholme, who was head of A&R at Sony by this time, asked me to work with him. Bow was signed to Death Row records, and the label was using him like their mascot in all their posters and flyers, but the kid was just languishing there. No one ever gave him the solo record he was promised. Snoop kept Bow under his wing, letting him rap as a featured artist on stuff, but then Snoop left Death Row.

His lil' protégé needed a new label home. Steve signed Bow

to Epic under Sony, so he was already on a sister label. I guess Bow's mom and everyone else involved with Bow's career were getting worried about what her child was being exposed to back on the West Coast. They were looking to make a switch to someplace that was more "kid-friendly." They also wanted to hook up with a producer who was successful with child rappers.

But at first I wasn't interested. "No way," I said. "I ain't taking on any more kiddie acts!"

"J.D., you can't pass on this kid," Steve said, and flew Bow down to Atlanta to meet me.

It was instant chemistry. The night Bow arrived happened to be my *1472* album release party at the Atrium. Me and Jay-Z were performing, then I introduced Lil' Bow Wow onstage to freestyle. Until then I'd never seen him perform except on a videotape. We couldn't get over what a lil' rhyming genius he was. Jay-Z was tripping on how Bow carried himself like a grown person. After Bow's first album was released, Jay-Z even paid Bow the highest compliment coming from a master rapper.

"Man, he talks better than fifty percent of the rappers who are adults out there," he said.

I was impressed. But from the get-go I could tell I had my work cut out for me. Like Usher, Bow Wow needed a guiding hand to help build his career. He needed to learn the business and work on his dance moves. He also needed some room to breathe and be a kid again. He was so small he looked more like an eight year old, but his big eyes looked like they'd seen some shit. His nails were bitten down to the quick like he had some real adult worries. His rapping had a real hard vibe considering his age, like he had an old soul. Snoop always insisted he made Bow leave the room when he smoked weed and stuff, but you never know.

Bow went back to his hometown in Ohio. By then I pretty much knew I wanted to sign him and the fact that he was at Sony was a perfect fit, but I wasn't satisfied with him being on another label. He had to be part of the So So Def family. That was one of my conditions. The Sony executives wanted to turn Bow into another Kris Kross success story badly enough that they agreed to my terms and made the swap from Epic to So So Def.

Pretty soon Bow was back in Atlanta. But I had some other conditions before I started working with him. His rhymes had to be clean and age-appropriate. No more cursing. Me and Bow's parents made a deal with him that he could stay in the music business only as long as he maintained good grades in school, and traveled with a private tutor when he was on tour. I hooked him up with my aunt, Lucy, the same woman who tried to tutor me back in the day.

Over at my mother's house Bow settled right in. As soon as he saw all the video games and toys he figured I was just a big kid. My crib was everything a boy like Bow could ever dream of.

"Ohmigod!" he said. "I thought you were some uptight preppy dude, but you're actually pretty cool!"

While we vibed together Bow wanted to do everything I was

doing and have all the toys and props I had. Like me at the time, he had cornrows. He learned my fashion sense and started wearing baggy clothes and Timberlands. He also picked up my demeanor. It was like I was rolling with Mini-Me!

Even now that Bow Wow's 19, Janet says she notices it more than ever. When he performs on TV she says he's 100 percent like me. From the way I talk to the way I move, he's like a mirror image.

That first Christmas he was with us in Atlanta, me and my mother practically adopted Bow. I gave him one of my iced-out chains, with a diamond-studded Mickey Mouse. It had 131 stones on it. His mother was upset because he didn't even want to leave Atlanta to come home on Christmas Eve. His stepdad had to come and get him.

Eventually we got to work on his first solo album, *Beware of Dog*. Bow was a funny lil' kid to work with. When he was on, he was on. But in between times he was a pain in the ass. Even worse than Brat.

When we were on the road, he egged the tour bus. One of his favorite tricks was to sneak into my Louis Vuitton backpack and steal all my jewelry, or hide it someplace where I couldn't find it for weeks.

One time he grabbed my diamond Cartier watch and a platinum-and-diamond chain worth a few hundred thou, put them on and dared me to take them off him. I had to chase him around the joint for hours. Another time he drove one of my sound engineers, Johnny, nuts, by hiding under one of the little cubicle desks out front and calling every extension in the building.

When he didn't feel like working it took a minute to motivate him. I had to pretty much drag him out of his bed when I needed him to record something in the studio.

"I'm just a kid, I'm too young to be doing this," he whined each time.

He said the exact same thing if he was on his PlayStation 2.

"Leave me alone, I'm just a kid!"

A couple of years later the studio rebellion got much, much worse. Bow can be one difficult motha to deal with. Even when he was a little kid he had a lot of anger. I should put a sign up on my studio door saying "The Doctor is IN" because half the time I work with artists like him, I feel like I'm their therapist.

Today, Bow's still got that little child in him despite all the stuff he's done in life. Even though he acts like a kid, he hates it when people treat him like one. He gets into these fits.

In 2001, when we were working on his second album, *Doggy Bag*, he started talking smack to my guys in the studio and they gave it right back to him and then some. He couldn't take it. He can't defend himself verbally in situations like that so he gets overwhelmed and goes totally crazy. He went on a tear and smashed up some of my favorite pieces of studio equipment. Then he grabbed some knives from the kitchen and started acting like he was gonna stab one of my sound engineers!

I came down hard on Bow for that. It was the first album we recorded in the 14,000-square-foot studio that Sony had just built for me, SouthSide. Everything was shiny, brand new and expensive, and Bow was on a tear to wreck it. No one's ever pissed me off so much. I kicked him out of the studio and called his mother.

"Bow's gonna be there in twenty minutes. Don't ask what he did but he's not coming back here," I said.

Bow got home in 15. Outside of the engineers at SouthSide I never told anyone what he did. For the next two weeks he called me every day to ask if he could come back to the studio but I wouldn't pick up his calls. Even though it set back our production schedule he had to learn his lesson. If anyone else had pulled that shit they'd have been banned for life!

But Bow wanted to work just as bad as any other star I've worked with. Despite all his issues he has that hunger for success. The first album sold three million units and the single, "Bounce With Me," was a major hit. Bow Wow entered into *The Guinness Book of World Records* as the youngest solo rapper to hit number one on the U.S. charts. The follow-up album, *Doggy Bag*, also went platinum.

I see the future in Bow Wow. He doesn't just have a sparkle, he has a laser beam coming out of him. He's one of the few artists with the potential to be another legend like Michael Jackson. He was also the closest thing I ever had to a son. I don't usually get as tight with an artist. I guess the relationship with Bow was special because when he first came to me he was so little and it was clear he needed me as a father figure as well as a producer. But just like in any close family, its members can hurt each other without even meaning to.

# 14

# SHAKE IT OFF

Good things and bad things in my life tend to come in waves. By 2002, I had everything: my main girl, my baby girl, a bunch of stars on my roster, and a hand in just about every major hit on the charts. But a tsunami was coming. It was time to pay up in more ways than one.

The music business ain't all about this fun, glamorous life that people think they see. Sometimes it's full of pain. I compare it to getting tattoos. If you want a fly piece of art on your body, the process can hurt like hell. But if you focus on how painful the needle is gonna be, you'll end up compromising and picking a tattoo that's too small or that's somehow wrong. The pain will overshadow the art. But after you go through it a couple of times you realize it's no big deal. That's how I got addicted.

I got my first tattoo when I was 19. When I saw how rock stars like Axl Rose and Tommy Lee were covered, that whole image caught me. My first one didn't turn out so good because I got scared of the needle and wimped out of a better design. It was just Popeye, but it was too small and the artist wasn't that good. I messed up on the second one too. Now every time I look at my right arm I say, "Oh, those are my mistakes."

When it's something that lasts forever you need someone who's good. I didn't even realize there were real artists making tattoos until I found someone, Mark Mahoney, who has a studio on the Sunset Strip in L.A. I let him do the rest. Now my neck, both my arms, triceps, back, shoulder blades, the tops of my legs and hands are covered. I'm not as inked-out as my buddy, Travis Barker, but I come close. I've got musical notes on my jugular, along with a rose twisted around my initials. I've got the Afroman, my So So Def mascot, inked on my right shoulder, and So So Def written out across the top of my back.

It's like I'm collecting so many tattoos as I go through life that my body is becoming a scrapbook. My child's face and name, Shaniah, are near my heart. I've also got a tattoo of Marlon Brando's head—who doesn't wanna be the Godfather? I've got a Chinese symbol for wealth on one hand and a Catholic cross on the other. Down one arm it says, "I do it all so well so those who don't like it can go to hell." One hand says "Number One," but the skin on your fingers is thin and it hurt so bad. There's a spider web on my elbow and a skull on my left forearm, for that hard rocker look. I may have to stop soon because I'm running out of body parts to tattoo!

It's harder for pigment to show up on brown skin, so the needle has to go in deeper and more often. It can be a bitch. You've got to think about the art, and how great the end result will be, and get past the pain. That's what I do in life. When something's worth doing I try to shake off the bad stuff and keep moving ahead.

Even though I was delivering hits, the love affair with Sony/ Columbia was turning stone cold. My dad tried to support me and fight for my needs at the label and for the first two years he was president of black music, things were running smoothly. Anything I wanted would pretty much get done. But when things were getting tense over my deal and I was bumping heads with the other executives, my dad said the fact that they made him an executive and had him report directly to Don Ienner put him in a difficult spot.

I guess in many ways his hands were tied. It was a case of divide, conquer, and neutralize. My father couldn't fight the power. You can only scream so much when you're inside. During certain conversations he said they even made him leave the room, claiming there could be a conflict of interest because of his relationship with me.

After three years, in 1998, they fired him. Even though my father was officially in charge of all black music, including my division, they didn't bother informing me of the personnel change. I was hurt. I couldn't understand why it didn't occur to

Don or Tommy Mottola to get on the horn and let me know I'd be reporting to some other urban music executive. It was as if they were saying, "Oh, J.D. doesn't matter, let his dad tell him what happened."

It was going sour for a long minute before I left. In 1999, I was the first producer in history to simultaneously hold the number one spots on three charts for three records, but no one gave me any props. I was the one making all the noise. I should have had a bigger situation. In my 10 years with the label, I never had an album not go platinum or multiplatinum. But it was like it was no big deal to them. It was just expected. I felt I had no voice up in New York even though I was still the one doing all the work.

That's partly because it's the nature of these joint-venture deals. The good thing is the label funds a big chunk of the over-head. The bad thing is you hit heads on the creative side. Differences of opinion over how projects were marketed were hurting my own label's overall direction and growth. They didn't support me in signing the artists I wanted to sign. They never put out Trina Broussard's album. It was partly her fault, but the label should have believed in it and done more. The writing was on the wall. Then, in 2001, we had a big fight.

Jagged Edge's last album under the deal, *Jagged Little Thrill*, would've blown up much bigger than it did if the label had listened to me. The single "Where the Party At," featuring Nelly, was an instant hit on rap, R&B, and pop radio. I knew that by putting Nelly on, it would give Jagged a much bigger audience outside of R&B and sell more records. I did a remix with myself, Bow Wow, and Brat to further prove my theory and I was right. But we needed to release a second single to stoke the fire and keep people interested by the time the album dropped.

But the label figured they'd just rely on the power of the remix. They were crazy. We had one of the biggest hits of the year but the album only sold a million copies because we didn't release another song soon enough. You can't have that kind of momentum and lose ground.

I've since learned it's typical of guys on the executive floor of a major label to operate like that. They'll promote a record, but they'll never do more than they have to if they aren't really feeling the artist like that. Jagged could have blown up so much bigger, but a label has to be really in love with the artist and Jagged's style just wasn't where the Sony and Columbia heads were at.

On some level I could understand their attitude toward me personally. A man can be married to the most gorgeous woman on the planet, but if he's been living with her and seeing her every day, he doesn't see it any more. He starts taking her for granted. That's how I felt—invisible.

Columbia caught me when I was just a kid and they still thought of me that way. Starting young and being one of the first to do that kind of a deal had its disadvantages. While I was grinding it out, I had to watch new guys come along and grab a bigger paycheck. I could see what was going on over at Arista. They were giving way more attention to L.A. with his deal than

Columbia and Sony were giving me. I knew because I had conversations with L.A. about it. I felt like Anakin Skywalker in *Revenge of the Sith* when the elder council members were dissing him. They didn't appreciate his powers or trust his judgment. It was time for things to get dark.

I called a meeting with my artists back at the So So Def headquarters in Atlanta. I had everyone in the conference room who was on my label, Brat, Jagged, and Xscape, along with their managers. Bow Wow was also there with his mom. My dad, all my producers, Eddie, and Diane McDonald were in the room too.

"I want y'all to know there's some stuff going down up in New York and I'm thinking about leaving the label," I told them.

Everyone gasped. "Why, what happened?" they said. I filled them in on some of my issues. I told them I couldn't tell them yet where I'd end up, but that I would take them with me if they were willing to go. I told them I knew in my heart it'd be someplace bigger, with a much larger deal that would give me the clout and control to make them more successful than they'd already been. But they had to trust me and I had to know where they stood.

"Are y'all with me?" I asked.

"Yeah! We're good! We all with you!" they said.

Seemed like we were cool. Everyone was on the same page. No one in that room expressed any doubt about our future together. No one said a word.

Meanwhile, behind the scenes, the powers at Sony were muscling up and deciding how big a check they could afford to write to steal everyone away from me. They were going through the back door to talk to my artists and cut me out of the conversation. With the exception of Brat, my loyal little sister, every single one of my performers went for the money.

The day I found out they were leaving me was one of the saddest days of my career. But I can't say I was all that surprised. Most of the time when you leave a label it's just not possible to take all your acts with you. The powers that be set the price too high. They want anywhere from $5 million to $10 million to release an artist from his contract. I didn't have that kind of money, and it wasn't likely that any other label I did a deal with would be willing to front that kind of change no matter how good my acts were.

Under the circumstances, I couldn't blame anyone in my So So Def family for choosing to stay with Sony and leave the fold. Xscape were already dissolving by themselves. Jagged had a lifestyle to support and performers come to rely on those fat advance checks from record labels. Most bury themselves in debt until the next wad of cash comes along.

I've been through ups and downs with all the artists I've developed from scratch. By record three, they usually start thinking their previous success was just how it's supposed to be and they start to get the itch to do it on their own or try out a different producer. Not only do they think they don't need me anymore, they start believing that I'm the one holding them back.

But my departure from Sony, and my artists' decision to stay, was nothing personal like that. It was just business, and on that level they had no choice.

But Brat was the exception. She chose to stay with me, despite the temptation of a big fat check. She's gone off to work with other producers, but I encouraged her to do it so she could learn how it goes in other studios. She always comes back, and even when I'm busy with other projects she waits her turn. Brat's so tied to me she has a tattoo on her right arm with both our names. When she got it she said, "J.D., you and me are stuck for life." That kind of loyalty is rare in artists. It's rare in anyone.

In some ways, Brat was more upset when everyone walked than I was. She even went on the radio to talk trash about the artists who left.

"J.D., I don't understand this, my feelings are hurt," she said. "We're a music family, we're like blood!"

"It's cool, Brat, let 'em leave," I said. "I got this."

It was true. I can see when things like this are gonna happen even before they go down. Like I knew what was gonna happen with Virgin months before it did. Those kids had a choice between nothing and knowing they had homes and money coming in. They were in the middle of their careers. I knew they'd leave. I was sad to lose what I'd built and break up the family, but I knew we'd cross paths again. I also knew I'd be able to sign up a whole new roster of talent, wherever I was going to next.

The only hard part was Bow Wow. He wasn't even 16 and he

didn't understand the nature of the business. He had a lot of grown-up people around him making decisions for him, and he had so many people in his ear telling him stuff that wasn't really true that he got confused.

When it came time to do Bow Wow's next album, *Unleashed*, Sony offered me only two songs as an outside producer. I was insulted. This was an artist I'd nurtured and built from scratch. I made him into a platinum-selling act, and that was all they were willing to give me? I felt like I should be making his whole record. I told them that I wouldn't do it on those terms. I guess they figured they could do better.

Lord knows what the people at Sony told Bow Wow. I know somebody told him I wasn't coming to the studio to work with him because I didn't want to have anything to do with his album. They left out a few essential details and made him believe it was something personal against him.

Bow Wow kept paging me but I didn't answer. Then he went through his people asking for me. When I paged them back I said, "Nah, I don't fuck wit that." I wasn't talking about Bow Wow. It was the whole situation with Sony and the lousy production deal they were offering me. But that's not how Bow took it.

Bow happened to see that page and took it in the worst way. He decided he was going to turn his whole album into an act of rebellion against me. Bow had that mind-set anyway. He was a teenager and trying to show his independence. He'd always brag, and still does, "J.D., I'm gonna be a better producer than you one day!"

Lil's signs of mutiny were all over the place. He used to get mad at me and sulk when I wouldn't let him come to the club with me because he was underage. Sometimes he showed up without me and got his bodyguard to sneak him in. He felt like he had to challenge me but he was just a teenager trying out his swagger. Deep down he was a kid who felt like he was losing a father figure after his real father had already abandoned him. The whole episode was hard on him in the worst way. He felt like he was left to go on his own.

*Unleashed* wasn't a success. That made Bow even more mad at me. "I hate J.D.!" he said in just about every media interview at the time. "I hate his guts!"

I kept my distance. At the time I didn't fully understand where all this hate was coming from. But when he was in L.A., almost two years later, filming his movie *The Johnson Family Vacation,* he came to see me at Janet's house in Malibu.

It seems my dad, who was still managing Bow Wow back then, set him straight on a few things that happened and Bow decided to do the grown-up thing and talk to me man-to-man.

"I was on an 'I hate Jermaine' campaign because I didn't know the full story," he told me. "People around me didn't want us together. I had people in one ear telling me one thing, and people in the other ear telling me something else. It was like I had to make a sudden right turn after so long walking a straight line."

By the next album, in 2005, there was no question we'd be a team again. Bow insisted to Sony executives that we be allowed to work together. This time the songs were about Bow as a young man and teen heartthrob. *Wanted* went platinum. The single "Fresh Azimiz" is one of my all-time favorites. At the time of writing this, Bow's latest album, *The Price of Fame*, was number two on the charts and his single, "Shortie Like Mine," stayed in the top 10 of the *Billboard* Hot 100 list for weeks. Musically, we're back on track. Bow's still young, but as an artist he's growing up.

I also became Bow's manager. Today we're friends. Bow told me he still sees me as his father figure and I guess it's inevitable. But I'm not letting myself get too caught up in that role. I wouldn't do that with any artist, because you never know when there's gonna be some twist that changes things up again. As tight as we are, what I am is his producer.

It wasn't just Bow Wow. All the artists who left me ended up coming back in some way or another, including my guys in Jagged Edge. Eventually they all realize it's not as much fun being on the outside, especially when others don't care like I do.

Brat was furious. She couldn't understand how I could talk to any of them again and agree to produce them. But she's more emotional than I am. She's just being a loyal little sister and doesn't get that business is just business.

After all that I've been through over the years, it's hard for people to trip me up. It takes a lot to really upset me. If somebody does get to me that deep, I might curse 'em on the low but I don't let anyone know it. I'm not one to pick fights. Instead of getting mad, I put the wall down and get even.

It happened a few months before everything fell apart at Sony, when I gave an interview to *XXL* magazine. They asked me who I compared myself to as a producer. I was getting so sick of that question. People always want to compare me to somebody. Nowadays, as president of a major label, people compare me to Jay-Z. That's the way the media is.

But I'm an original. I've been doing my thing since long before other big hip-hop producers. It's just that I chose to stay in Atlanta. I wasn't in New York promoting myself because I want more people to come to the South. Being in the ATL is my whole meaning in life. My whole career, I preferred grinding in my own studio, spending more time actually producing hits than frontin' on the East or West Coasts for the world to see.

So I reacted to the interviewer's question by going into my cocky lil' Don Chi Chi mode. Don Chi Chi was the Mafia dude who was willing to take out the head guy, and that's what I've always aimed to do in my career—take over the industry and be the best. That's my mentality, music-wise.

"Whether it be Puff or anybody that people wanna call my competition, I will take them out," I said. "Hands down, ain't nobody in the industry that can do what I do. Not Dre, not Timbaland, not nobody."

Hell, if I don't cheerlead for myself, who else will? I only meant it in a playful way. I talk smack like that with my closest friends. I'm competitive with everybody. I'm always looking to see who can put out the most hits. But I'm a fan of everybody's work. I had nothing but respect for Dr. Dre. I still do. He's a leader. I feel he's the best hip-hop producer out there. What I was saying was that what I do is different. I'm not really like any of these guys. I do R&B, hip-hop crossover stuff in my own unique way. Ain't nobody can touch that!

Dre twisted what I said and got all heated about it. He and his friends took it to a place it didn't need to go. He called me "Papa Smurf" and "Mini-Me" in some dis song he wrote called "What You Say." He called me a midget and said he was gonna step on me!

Timbaland also had something to say, telling me I could put my lips where the sun don't shine. Then their buddy Eminem felt he had to chime in, calling me a "gay midget."

They were crazy remarks. I wasn't really hurt by the barbs being thrown my way. I can take a joke about my stature. If anything, I found the references to midgets funny. When I was a kid, my favorite movie was *Under the Rainbow* and I've been tickled by little people ever since.

I've got a picture of me and Verne Troyer, the guy who played Mini-Me in the Austin Powers movies, on prominent display in my studio. The two of us are doing a one-fingered salute for the camera. Eddie can tell you the one time in my life I laughed the hardest was when we were on line in the Dairy Queen when a family of midgets came in. I don't know where they came from, but we cracked up so much we had to leave without our burgers. I'm not real proud of that, but I just couldn't help myself.

I said a few things in the press to defend myself when I realized everyone was bugging out over that interview. But after the second and third record from Dr. Dre and his crew, I couldn't let the dis storm continue. This all started early on in 2002 and was still going on months later. I got so tired of hearing about it I decided to do a little freestyle. It didn't even have a name. It was just my thought one night. I decided to use Ice Cube's flow from "Jackin' for Beats," over some of Dre and Timbaland's tracks. It went like this:

> *Gimme dat beat fool, it's a full-time jack move*
> *Fuck y'all I make the motherfucking track move*
> *And Eminem, Tim, Tom, Dick and Hank*
> *Already know that I'm something y'all ain't*
> *A little young non-stopper*
> *And from Rap to R&B I'm breaking niggas off proper*
> *With that S-O S-O DEF M-O-B; fuck Dre, this J.D.*
> *And here's how I'm a greet ya*
> *Stop . . . fool—come off that beat*
> *Ya should've never fucked with College Park*
> *You little gay ass mark*
> *All you can say is that I'm short*
> *But my dough is long*
> *Dr. Dre motherfucker come on*
> *See I know you don't do half the work in the studio*
> *Plus I heard you like letting niggas play with your booty*
> *    hole*

It was circulated over the Internet and got some airplay on radio in Los Angeles, where Dre is from. Jay-Z was surprised. He paged me and said, "I thought you weren't a rapper!" It's true. That whole tradition of rapper beefs has never been our way in the South. But I had to stand up for myself.

That was my last word on the subject. I'm sure those guys got their laughs in later, when I was raided by the IRS.

That whole situation was a bunch of issues in my life coming to a head. On one front, I pretty much made myself a target with that whole "Money Ain't a Thang" swagger. There was one tax agent in particular who didn't approve of the way I was kickin' it. The problem was I wasn't getting information sent to me that should have been sent to me. No one was telling me that I was being watched or that I owed money. It got even worse when Jan bought me a big white Hummer for my birthday. The IRS must've thought, "Oh, he can't afford to pay his taxes but he's buying himself a new car?!"

Next thing I knew this agent showed up at my studio door with a news channel camera crew and the police. I guess it was a great story for the media. Imagine the headlines: MR. MONEY AIN'T A THANG CAN'T PAY HIS TAXES! The press had a field day at my expense, although most of what they reported was wrong.

Janet was with me at the time. I remember being scared they were going to seize my whole studio and all the equipment. That's the one thing that would have really hurt me because it would have stopped me from working for a minute. But they couldn't touch it because technically at the time it was still Sony property.

One policeman was allowed to walk through the studio while everyone else waited outside. Some people assumed from seeing the police at my door that I was being arrested. I decided to play it cool and put out the red carpet. The police were respectful and even looked embarrassed to be there.

The IRS agent handed me a $2.5 million bill for the tax period ending in 1998. I just took the notice and said, "Okay."

The press reported that I lost a bunch of cars, jewelry, and computer equipment. But to my surprise and relief, they didn't take much. The IRS raided both my houses and got some furs, some paintings, and one car, but that was about it. They didn't need to seize my property because it was just a second before I handed them a check for the full amount owed.

There was some back-and-forth about the exact amount on the bill. We'd already been paying off Inland Revenue in installments and the final tally wasn't as high as they said. But I have to admit, I messed up. My accountants weren't overseeing my finances properly. So So Def's last distribution deal with Sony and Columbia didn't leave us with enough cash flow to cover our overheads. By 2000, we went way over our budget after spending about $5 million to build SouthSide.

Meanwhile me, my dad, and everyone else involved in running So So Def were dipping into the pot and overspending. I decided to take a hard look at everyone who was, or I should say wasn't, handling business, and trace all the problems I was facing with the tax man back to the source. It was a wake-up call. I fired a bunch of people, including my dad.

I can't really blame my father. He's not directly responsible and he was never in charge of paying my bills. But it's a lesson for a lot of kids coming up in this business. They get caught up in the money while failing to handle their business and pay attention to the details. It's always tempting to come off all fly and flashy, but it gets us the wrong kind of attention from the IRS and it's no way to run a business.

It was all on me. I was responsible. I was so into the creative side of being a producer that I left the handling of the business side of my business to other people. When my dad left Sony I put him in charge of my label. It was an old habit of mine, letting my father manage the stuff that distracted me from what I do in the studio. I made him chief of operations, but you can give people any title you want to; if they don't have a stake, they're not going to be responsible for anything.

I still love and respect my father. He put me here and gave me my first exposure to the music business, and in a lot of ways he's helped me over the years. But as far as the company was concerned he wasn't accountable. It was time to end our business relationship and just be father and son.

The episode was one of the worst experiences I've been through but it made me realize that nobody else at So So Def matters but me. I'm the boss. Once again I had to man up. I needed to get myself in a position where if I was going to be the fall guy let me be the fall guy. I don't want anyone else pretending to be what they're not. It was my money that was being spent. If things got really bad and I couldn't come back from it everyone else would be tripping and going off their merry way but me.

I took a few hard knocks over the years when it came to choosing the wrong partner. To build my brand I tried starting new businesses a few times. For a spell I had a sports management company and a fashion label I called Dupri Style. They failed because I trusted people to run things who didn't have enough skin in the game and were looking to make a fast buck.

I made the same mistake when I started my restaurant, Café Dupri, in Buckhead, two years ago. The idea to have a restaurant first came a few years earlier when I was at Quincy Jones's house, and he was telling me how sick Ray Charles was.

"You know, if you would have eaten better and paid closer attention to your health . . . ," they told him. Ray's health was falling apart. Years of drug abuse didn't help. But if he'd gone to the doctor regularly, exercised, and ate right—something too few black men do—he wouldn't have so much wrong with him. It wasn't long after that Ray died.

Something spoke to me that day. I was drinking a six-pack of Dr Pepper and eating fried stuff like Wendy's burgers every day. I wasn't even 30 and I was feeling sluggish. It was no coincidence that somebody was trying to tell me, "J.D., you've got a chance right now. Clean it up. Stop eating all that junk food. You running around too much." I decided it was so important to start eating healthy that I had to open my own restaurant and do it my way.

I hooked up with a guy who owned a deli in the area I liked called Goldberg's Bagel Co. I wanted it to be a 24-hour place like Elmo's in New York. But right away the problems started. I spent double what he said it was going to cost. I was already a little disturbed because the café was a lot more high-end than I wanted it to be. He also talked me into getting a liquor license, and put it in his name. Then he started trying to fight me on the healthy menu.

After a while, when things fell way behind schedule but the bills kept coming in, I could see the place was turning into a money pit. Good dollar after bad was going down a big black hole. I guess the bagel guy thought my dough is so long I wouldn't even notice. But he didn't realize I'm smarter than I seem. I decided to end our partnership. I didn't like the way he was taking care of the business.

His way of paying me back was to take the liquor license with him, and put the word out to make it seem like I had a problem with the city. It became a big story in Atlanta. I guess he thought his move would put me in a position where I would stress out and close the restaurant. But I didn't care. I was glad to be rid of him even if it took a few more months to get a new license. Nowadays Café Dupri is doing just fine.

These days I trust no one. Not with my record company, anyway. I've been burned too many times. I can't go away for a month and expect anyone else to look after things at So So Def.

It would all fall apart. I'm not saying my people would deliberately mess things up. I just mean they wouldn't own it.

These setbacks were all good lessons for me. Especially the tax raid. It taught me that I had to handle my business and focus more on what was happening inside the company. I wasn't too worried about the money. I knew I had a multimillion-dollar label deal with Arista right around the corner. L.A. Reid, my old friend, rival, and mentor, was running things over there, and he gave me my first executive position at a major label, as a senior vice president. That meant the tax man could take his cut straight out of my paycheck!

Each bad thing that happened to me in 2002 made me stronger. I realized that no one could push me. When they try I don't fret. I'm too quick, like mercury. Try grabbing the liquid from a broken thermometer and you'll soon learn you can't do it. When someone tries to hold me down, I just move my ass out of the way and reposition myself. I'm 10 steps ahead of the guy who wants to get one over. He can't touch me. Hell, he can't even catch me!

# 15

# UNFINISHED

This last chapter is anything but. At 34 years old as I write this, I'm at the beginning of a whole new phase and there's no telling how it's going to play out. There's so much shit going down in my life right now that my writing can't keep up with the present. It takes months between handing in a book to a publisher and getting it to print. Since I can pack years' worth of livin' into just a few weeks, a lot of things you already heard about in the press won't be in this book. That's why I'm calling this chapter "Unfinished." This story is open-ended because it has to be.

What I can tell you is that things are gonna be different. Even from the time I started writing the first chapter, I've noticed some interesting shifts in my world. Until about two years ago, few people knew who I really was. As a producer, the invisibility has always been okay with me. More professional recognition would have been a nice extra. But as long as I could continue to do what I do and make money at it, I never much cared about the fame.

But by early 2006, I started seeing myself show up more in places like *People* magazine and *The New York Times* as something other than Jan's arm candy. It put me in mind to conduct a small experiment and test out a theory. That spring I went on vacation to Mexico. I needed to give my brain a rest after months working in the studio on Janet's new album. Before I left, I bought myself a lil' something that cost about as much as three cars, and with the extra time on my hands to relax and reflect I got to thinking about what it all meant.

I paged a friend and asked her to slip a story about my new trinket to *The New York Post*'s "Page Six" column. She said I was crazy; there was no way even the *Post* would print something that trivial. I wasn't so sure they would either. But they did! People were trippin' over it. I got calls from other celebrity magazines, like *Us Weekly*, which even did their own follow-up story. It just goes to show the more stupid something is the more people want to read about it.

Along with the attention came some other shit. I caught so much flack for it, my pager blew up with friends saying, "Say it ain't so!" An older, very high-up guy in the music industry, I won't say who, even felt he had to lecture me about not wasting my money and investing more in my own business. I told him, respectfully, that when he was my age he was allowed to have his fun, right or wrong, and he should let me do the same.

The whole petty "Page Six" thing triggered enough deep thinking about where I was at this point in my life that I wrote a poem. I called it, "Live the Life."

*Maybe I'm not doin' the right thing*
*Maybe I'm not in the right place*
*But I'm livin' life*
*So full that everybody around me wants a taste*
*Maybe I shouldn't be takin' this*
*Maybe I shouldn't be drinkin' that*
*But I can't tell cause everybody's trying to get where I'm at*
*I prob'ly shouldn't have bought that*
*I prob'ly shoudn't be goin' here*
*But I constantly hear people around me sayin' if I was you I*
  *wouldn't even care*
*I bought a pair of 300k dollar earrings and people flipped*
*I take um out to clean um, look an' just trip*
*'Cause I remember when I had jewelry from the flea market*
*But now I'm buyin' stuff some people think is retarded*
*If I ain't livin' the life I don't know whatchu call it*
*I'm somethin' like a 34-year-old ballaholic*
*If I end up broke so be it*
*I done lived my life and seen it: how niggas wish they could*
  *see it*
*Been with a lotta dimes*
*And ended up with the baddest*
*Always smilin' I could never be the saddest*

*'Cause I've been livin' my life since 1992*
*And whether right or wrong that's what uma continue to do*

That test with the *Post* gave me the answer I was looking for. Even the smallest piece of news I put out about myself could get attention. Don't get me wrong. I see this for what it is. People should never get caught up in their own hype. Fame can be a dangerous and destructive thing if you allow it to get too personal. But when you recognize what it is and use it with the appropriate cynicism, it gives you real power in the music industry.

It doesn't matter how hard you work. The more retarded stuff people print about you in the newspaper, the more people are impressed and the more business you can command. Artists want to sign with you or be produced by you, radio and TV stations want you to come and talk about your acts; promoting records, clothing lines, whatever, becomes that much easier. I respect Puffy for figuring that out sooner than I did.

I call the kind of fame you can get through the media "the Force." That's sort of how Anakin became Darth Vader in *Revenge of the Sith*. He figured out how to use his power and bend it to his will. When I first saw that movie it felt like I was on Ecstasy. The whole place just lit up for me at that moment Anakin realizes who he really is. Everyone around me must've thought I was on drugs too when I said out loud, "That's me! I'm Anakin!"

Episodes One, Two, and Three of the *Star Wars* series finally came alive for me. I was a fan. But this time I felt a whole new connection between my life and that movie. The more people, like label executives or music journalists, frustrate me, the more pissed off I get, the more I'm going to think about what it takes for me to be Darth Vader and start killing people!

Of course, I mean that in the sense of killing the charts. My way of being a danger to others is to own every hit that's out there. I can make it bad for people. I can make it so that if you want to put out a record that's successful, you have to go through me. The city of Atlanta is like that already. It's like the Sith Lord. People used to be embarrassed to say they were from the South, but today you can't make an urban record without coming here. You might try, but before you get to the end of that album, some producer from Atlanta is gonna get a call.

When one city controls the whole momentum of the industry, that's the power of the dark side, that's the revenge of the Sith at work! Dr. Dre proved you don't have to go to New York to make a record, you can go to L.A. But the new producers like me and Dallas Austin prove you have to come to the South. Atlanta IS Motown, and cities like New Orleans are its satellites. And it's never gonna stop. The South is where our ancestors are from. As far as urban music is concerned, everyone is coming home.

I don't have the same control over the industry my city has, but I believe one day, maybe next month, maybe next year, I'm gonna get there. People are gonna have to acknowledge my power. I've got everyone from La Toya to Lionel Richie to Enrique Iglesias coming to me for hits. I never stop working, but I can't even think about slowing down right now. When it gets to the point where at least 80 percent of the songs in the top 10 are mine, that's when I'll stop.

The power's been taking its time to build. I've been "the kid" in the music business my whole life. It was only when L.A. hired me and I got with Arista in the beginning of 2003, that I finally felt the respect of a major record label.

Making me a senior executive gave me a say in decisions that were made at the top that I never had before. I didn't want to fail at it. I wanted to learn how to play the corporate game from the inside so I could take over the top spot at a major label one day. L.A. was my direct report, and he sat me down and coached me. He explained everything about what label management really meant. He taught me how to navigate the politics. He also gave me a little lecture I'll never forget.

"It's very simple," he said. "All I expect of you is to do what you do best: Make hits, make hits, make hits. As many as you can have coming out at the same time the better. Don't ever turn your back on where a hit may come from. Bring me something. Let me hear music. Tell me what you are doing today, who you are working on now, and what record is next. I want to know who's hot, who's not, what's the latest sound. Hits, hits, hits! That's all that really matters."

I soaked up everything he had to say like a sponge. L.A. wanted me to know the corporate bullshit about legalities and finance so I could better work the system. But he didn't want me to get caught up in it. He wanted me to stay focused on the music. Our business isn't really based on business. People get sucked in by meetings and corporate politics, but that doesn't sell records. A successful label isn't based on what happens in the boardroom. It depends on whatever is going on in popular culture right now.

Berry Gordy was one of the all-time greats in the music business, not because he aspired to own a corporation but because he aspired to be the head of a creative empire. No matter how rough things got with competition stealing artists and producers, Motown always had them beat because Berry Gordy always had at least half a dozen artists lined up and ready to put out the next hit single.

That's what I always aimed to do. Dominating the charts is what drives me. After that rough exit from Columbia, L.A.'s advice confirmed what my gut was already telling me. I could win the game. I knew the formula for making hit records, and this time I'd have the muscle to help them sell like they should.

I continued to work behind the scenes. L.A. was the CEO and the face of the label, but he put me in charge of black music. Arista was a pop label at the time, but the fact that urban artists knew me meant I could be a magnet for them and build up that part of its roster. It was during that brief period we did Usher's *Confessions* album. I also signed J-Kwon, Bone Crusher, and Anthony Hamilton. L.A. calls Anthony my "best signing." It was probably my easiest.

Anthony sang at some pre-Grammy breakfast for members of the music industry and my father caught his act. The dude was dressed all scruffy with no haircut and a toothpick in his mouth. He wanted to be the direct opposite of what everyone thinks is cool.

But his music and voice are so soulful and unusual that he caught everyone by surprise. My dad called me and told me to check him out and when I did I signed him on the spot. As a person, he's so country and real you don't mess with that. All I had to do was let him sing and put out his record. It doesn't get much simpler.

The golden spell at Arista didn't last long. Even though L.A. cleaned up at the Grammys in 2004 and could claim hit after hit with OutKast and Usher, they fired him and he went over to Def Jam. I didn't want to stay at Arista without L.A., but the shine I got from my success at Arista and my track record of hits got me plenty of offers for a new label home. I decided to go to Virgin because, at the time, they were prepared to make me president and let me run the whole show for their urban music division.

People said I was crazy. Of all the top four labels, Virgin was at the bottom. It'd been a long while since they put out any hits. Their last number one on the *Billboard* Hot 100 was Janet's song "All For You" and that was in 2001. Their last urban hit was Mariah's "Loverboy" that same year.

When they announced my appointment, my pager blew up with people asking: "For real? Are they still in business?"

But that's why I liked the idea. Here was a label that really needed me. In R&B they had well under 2 percent of the market share; in rap they owned about half a percent. When I got offered the job by Matt Serletic, Virgin's CEO at the time, and his deputy Larry Mestel, an old friend I worked with before, they told me I'd have the whole lane to myself. The urban music stage was all mine to build from scratch. I came on board because I vibed with them and knew they'd let me run things my way.

When I got there, it was even worse than I thought. Inside the building it was like a morgue. There was no life in there. People clocked in but I didn't see anyone working. I didn't hear no demos blaring on the sound system or phones ringing off the hook. I put a sign on my door saying, "J.D. is in the mother-fuckin' house!" to let people know I was there and to shake things up. I wanted them to feel they could come through my door. But it was like landing on a planet full of drones. It was on me to catapult Virgin into a young, hip label with chart-topping success in a market they never had before. More on that later.

People didn't think I could pull it off. You can count on one hand the number of young black executives at the top of the major labels: me, Kevin Liles, and Jay-Z. It's rare that we get this kind of shot at the top of the corporate ladder and there's a built-in expectation that we won't make it. It just drives us even harder to succeed.

I've been through so much already, I know I can handle the doubters. Last year I was at a brunch in Santa Barbara and a preacher came up to me and said something I'll never forget:

"People feed pigeons and throw stones at eagles."

At first I didn't know what to think. It was a little freaky. But the fact that he chose that particular time to say that to me meant something. I'd been feeling underappreciated for a while, so what he was saying touched me. He meant that when you don't stand out and you're just common like some pigeon, people will either leave you alone because you're dirty or take pity on you because you're needy and hungry. But when you're something rare and powerful who people don't understand, they wanna take you out because you're a threat, or catch you like some prize. It was like he was telling me to just keep doing what I was doing and my time would come.

The recognition really started to kick in after I wrote and produced songs on Mariah's big comeback album, *The Emancipation of Mimi*. One song in particular, "We Belong Together," made music history with more radio play than any other record since Elvis Presley and the Beatles.

That hookup came through L.A. Reid. After Virgin paid Mariah off for $28 million, Kevin Liles signed her to Def Jam, but then he left for Warner Music Group. Except for *Charm Bracelet* in 2002, an album I produced that did pretty well, she was left to drift for a minute. People figured it was all over for her after the "Glitter" disaster. But you don't write off talent like that.

L.A. knew it. Mariah's next big album was high on his list the second he moved over to Def Jam. He was one of the few people who could still see what she was capable of. He remembered what me and Mariah did together almost a decade earlier on "Always Be My Baby," and loved it. Even though I'd already moved on to Virgin, L.A. wanted me to work on her next album.

From the first beats to the final demo version we had just a few hours to get the whole record done. Mariah came to me this time, but she was the one on the night shift. She was scheduled to show up at 10:30 but she didn't get to Atlanta until 1 A.M. When she walked into SouthSide, she was all laid back, happy, and cracking jokes. People don't realize how much fun she is.

The whole thing went so fast. First the two of us sat down and discussed a couple of ideas. Then I brought in Johnta Austin into the conversation. That was a small feat. Mariah doesn't like working with writers she doesn't know, but I sorta snuck him in. As soon as she realized how good he is, she was cool.

Johnta's a songwriter who I produce now as an artist. But I wasn't feeling Johnta when I first met him. I wasn't down with having another songwriter around me. I wanted to be the only one. But not only was he persistent, he was good. I grew to like him out of respect. Musically we're so on the same page that having him as a permanent fixture at So So Def has allowed me to branch out and do even more.

The songwriting went smoothly, but, musically, me and Mariah had some back-and-forth. At first Mariah was pushing for something more ghetto.

"No it's too out there, too urban," I said. "Lean it more to-wards the middle."

I didn't want her doing all the syrupy ballad stuff her past label executives tried to push her into. She also needed to hold herself back from trilling up and down the scales. I wanted to keep the power of her voice inside the framework of a great song. We finally agreed on what she called a "thugged out ballad."

People say Mariah's a diva, all bossy and controlling, but I never noticed that side of her inside the studio. We have different styles of working. If a TV's on in a room she has to turn it off, and other artists, their crews, and their girlfriends are all banned from SouthSide when she's in the building. I respect her wishes. But musically she always meets me halfway. She wants the right record and so do I.

The song ended up being completely different from our original idea. By 5.30 A.M. we knew we had our hit single. I had to sing half of the end of the song because she wouldn't get on the plane without me finishing the lyric. I told her I didn't want to—like I said I hate singing in front of my artists—but she wouldn't leave until I did it.

When it was time for her to go home and record, I gave her my pep talk, "You've gotta sing the song full voice. Just do you and sing. People are gonna love you!" But she didn't even need me to say it. She was outta there by 6 A.M.

Mariah's a career artist. She'll be cranking out hits long after the pop tarts' careers finish up. When that whole album came out with all its hits—"We Belong Together," "Get Your Number," "Shake It Off," "What It Look Like," "Don't Forget About

Us"—people were looking at her like, "Yo, she came back!" But she just did what she's always done. She had a good song and sang her heart out. She can't tell me, "J.D. you're a lifesaver." I don't look at it like that. I just helped her remember who she was.

Pretty soon after the single, "We Belong Together," dropped, there was buzz. I was in my car, driving around Atlanta when I heard it on the radio, and a few minutes later my man Big Jon Platt, the guy who took Steve Prudholme's place at EMI Publishing, called me.

"You know, you really are a great songwriter," he said. "You're gonna be eating off that joint for the rest of your life!"

"Big Jon, you just made my day!"

From the beginning, people were talking about how that song would sweep up at the 2006 Grammys. But I wasn't gonna go there. Everyone said I'd win for best songwriter or producer for all the work I did on Usher's *Confessions* album the year before, and when it didn't happen I got disappointed.

Ever since then I made a point of not having too much faith in Grammy decisions. People said it was political because I resigned from the Academy after they dissed Janet, but that wasn't 100 percent the case. Most of the people who said I should win weren't even members who are making the decisions. It's a clean vote. That's what trips everyone out, because that's not usually the way in this business.

But the people who vote tend to skew older and whiter than today's real music market, like the vast majority of executives at a major record label. Just because a song is hot and breaks re-cords for sales and radio spins, it doesn't guarantee an award. I told myself I'd rather have the unit sales than some lil' statue. I'm more interested in defending my undefeated title of ASCAP Songwriter of the Year!

People were screaming even louder for me to get best pro-ducer in 2006 and I didn't even get a nomination. But it matters more to me how my artists are viewed, and whether they are having a good time. Then again, it might've been reverse psy-chology—a case of me psyching myself so that if I didn't win I wouldn't be going out of my mind!

But for Mariah's sake I was nervous. I really did hope this album would win something. We were nominated eight times and she'd been through so much since her last Grammy win. A few nods for her from an industry that wrote her off would've been cool.

The whole evening passed like a blur. It was exciting at first, then things fizzled out fast. I decided to skip the preshow stuff and turn up at the last minute. I was in slow motion that day. Janet wasn't coming. It's a boring show to sit through if you haven't been nominated.

I'm not crazy about red carpeting without my girl. I didn't want to have to go into Mr. Janet Jackson mode and answer all those dumb questions they like to ask me about her when she's not there. I wanted the focus to be on Mariah.

Our three awards were announced before the televised part of the show. Just as I pulled up I found out me and Johnta got one for best R&B song. To this day Mariah swears the Grammy for best R&B song means the most to her, because it's the first time she's been recognized more as an urban singer than a pop star and it was the category she always wanted to win.

"J.D., I'm satisfied," she said. "That's exactly what I was trying to do on this record."

We left the show when it was obvious the best song award was going to go to U2. It was crazy to me that the show's producers wouldn't let Mariah have her lil' moment up on stage. It was like she got all decked up for nothing. A lot of people were unhappy she didn't get her shine. In my opinion, it was just a bad decision they made.

Mariah's the queen. She went to a lot of trouble and invested in all these dresses for the occasion. This woman sold more records than anybody, more than 200 million worldwide, and the viewers didn't get to see her give her acceptance speech. That's why the Grammy show's ratings are down. People are tuning into *American Idol* instead because they know they're not gonna get to see what they want to see at the Grammys. But through it all, MC kept on smiling.

I couldn't wait to start celebrating. We planned the after party of all after parties at billionaire Ron Burkle's mansion in Bel-Air. Every A-lister in town was there: Eddie Murphy, Jay-Z, Chris Tucker, Gabriel Union, Mischa Barton, Kelly Clarkson, Joaquin Phoenix, Britney Spears, Rob Thomas, you name it. You couldn't get a better guest list. There were 600 people. We sent them the details of a secret location on these special LG phones we gave out to our invitees. Everyone was excited to see what would happen.

When we got there someone was choking and an ambulance came. Police were hassling people at the bottom of the driveway. Even Quincy Jones couldn't get in at first. Inside the music was turned down low, like it was a memorial service or something, not a hot Grammy after party. I took over the DJ booth and cranked the music up to get things started, but before anything could happen the cops and the fire marshal came and shut us down!

That sort of said it all. It was definitely going to be one of those nights. It was just a big anticlimax. I've never seen people spend the type of money we spent—damn near $1 million—in someone's $40 million house, only to have the party end before it even got started. If it had been at my crib that shit never would have happened. Somebody in L.A. was definitely hating on us that night!

Still, I got my Grammy. I finally knocked down one of my goals. Winning did mean something after all. As a true musician a Grammy is the ultimate reward. In this industry people don't pay attention to all that you do over the years. You know how hard you work and deep down you want that recognition. It helps feed the force.

A Grammy marked this era of my life and the comeback of Mariah Carey. The trophy is a signature of what happened, so no one can forget that 2006 is the year I did that record and won my first. I started building a shelf in my house, because it won't be the last.

Not that I've had any time lately to sit back and enjoy the moment. Winning a Grammy for a Mariah song did nothing for Virgin. The pressure was always on. People were expecting me to crank out hits within just a few months of joining the label. I was expecting the same thing from myself. But that's hard to do when you're starting with nothing. I had to find some new talent quick.

It didn't take long. Me and Bow Wow were at a car show in Dallas hosted by an Atlanta DJ, Greg Street, from V-103, the radio station where I do my show, when I first met the guys from Dem Franchize Boyz: Maurice Gleaton, a.k.a. Parlae, Bernard Leverette, a.k.a. Jizzal Man, Jamall Willingham, a.k.a. Pimpin, and Gerald Tiller, a.k.a. Buddie. Those guys were pure street and proud of it. They first met up in high school and started rhyming together. From the beginning they were all about representing the West Side of Atlanta. They set out to define a new wave of music and show everyone their version of pimping, clubbing, and living.

Their specific way of painting a picture caught me. They could bring the underground to So So Def, and I could bring them more into the mainstream and turn them into a national craze.

I'd already seen a video they put out for their single "White Tee." I decided I really liked their way of dancing and showing the lifestyle. That song became an anthem for the summer of 2004. Everyone started wearing big white tees.

I was so impressed I even did my own little remix of the song and it was playing all over radio. Me and DFB performed

it two or three times at the car show and the response got crazier and crazier each time.

"What's up, J.D.?" they said. "We really liked that remix. It's
a go! It's happening!"

I asked them what they had planned next. They were signed
to Universal/Motown on a one-shot deal with an option to do
another record, but it was taking the label a minute to do anything with them. I told them they had to find a way to pump it
up fast and get out the next record. They said they were free for
me to sign, so I swiped them up.

Their other single, "I Think They Like Me" was hot on the
streets of Atlanta, but I had a way to blow it up even bigger. I
was already planning to put out a compilation CD, *Young, Fly
and Flashy* for Virgin, to showcase some of the up-and-coming
talent I had on So So Def. I did a remix of DFB's song with
myself, Brat, and Bow. It became another summer anthem.

I started my career building acts from scratch. But I signed
these guys because they were already hot. When I find artists
with their own talent and style, I've learned to just kinda play it
back so I don't influence them too much. I probably did make
them better in some ways, but all I had to do was expose their
talent to the world. They were already sitting on something.

What I like most about these dudes is that they're not afraid
of the grind. They know how to work the strip clubs and the
dance clubs to make things hot in the street. I don't have to tell
them how to promote themselves. They already understand this
is a business.

By the time we did our first full album together under So So Def and Virgin, *On Top of Our Game*, things clicked into place just the way I like it. I didn't need to spend my time on instruction because they already had it. When we released their two singles, "Lean Wit It, Rock Wit It" and "Ridin' Rims," they went straight to the top. So did the Monica single I put them on, "Every Time Tha Beat Drop." I even put them on Mariah's remix of "Say Something."

By the summer of 2006, with the help of DFB, I gave Virgin EMI their first real chart action in years. Bubba Sparks had a top 10 hit, DFB had two number ones and Janet's single "Call On Me" was number one on the R&B charts. I quadrupled their market share in rap, and more than doubled it in R&B.

That success isn't counting all the other side projects I worked on at EMI that went platinum, including the hit single "Pullin' Me Back" by Chingy for Capitol Records. That was special. When we first met he told me he wanted to get with me since the Kris Kross days and be the third member. When "Pullin' Me Back" went to number one he sent me a page to tell me how much he appreciated what I did for him. Not many artists think to do it. They just believe their success was meant to be.

People ask me why I don't concentrate on producing more artists who are signed to So So Def, including my So So Def artists who are waiting their turn. Even my right hand Diane McDonald gives me a hard time about this. But in the long run becoming the go-to producer for everyone from R&B artists to rap stars is good for everyone at my label. It gets our name out there and helps create a movement. It's another way of feeding the power.

Virgin didn't make it easy though. I might have had my own lane but their traffic moves slow and the potholes never got fixed. Hiring one person doesn't solve the problem at a label like that until the deadweight employees who've created the dysfunctional culture are cut loose and replaced with people who know what hard work is. I'm not saying everyone had to be fired, but when I came in it was supposed to be the beginning of a whole new system and some of the existing employees weren't real happy about adapting.

For a year and a half I played tug-of-war with people who weren't looking to change. They were still a pop label that thought they just have to put out a record and see if it floats or sinks on the strength of who the artist is. They got rid of Matt Serletic and replaced him with another pop guy who doesn't know the urban landscape. No one had a clue about promoting, marketing, and distributing records in a way that connects to real consumers in the street. But they didn't wanna learn either.

I was on the phone 10 times a day having conference calls about the most basic shit. I had to explain that you can't put a record out a month or more later in Europe. These kids are on the computer every minute. In urban music the computer IS the street and you insult the consumer when they know you're putting them second.

Virgin was so out of the loop it was crazy. They needed to be in the clubs, getting with DJs, building buzz on the street and underground. Some kid with a MySpace site could do a better job of promoting his record than they did with all their millions. Their whole life is built on "let's put a record out, pray to God it works, then sit around and make every excuse why a record doesn't work when it doesn't sell."

They paid attention to the obvious. Music that has no substance, just pretty girls with long blond hair, that's pop music to them. Talent doesn't matter. Their way is 20 years out of date. Pop music isn't a destination, great music is the goal. My music starts out as R&B or hip hop and becomes pop music on the strength of what's playing in the clubs and on radio. Pop is what kids are paying attention to, and these days that's urban music.

The way they put out Janet's 2004 album, *Damita Jo*, reinforces my point. They had Kanye West work on her first single, but he didn't know anything about why Janet Jackson is Janet Jackson. You have to respect a career artist and understand everything that came before. Virgin wasn't showing any respect to Jimmy Jam and Terry Lewis by doing this. That's a big musician's gap right there. Kanye samples records. These guys play instruments. The creativity and sound of the record is going to be completely different. You don't just slap any hot young producer on a star like that. All they were thinking was "Janet needs to be fresh, let's get Kanye!"

Executive producing Jan's next record, *20 Y.O.* was the most important thing I had to do at Virgin. It was the last album under her contract. I was determined they were gonna get it right this time. I wanted them to have a hit despite themselves.

I never felt so much pressure on a project in my life. Janet's my girl but I was also kinda her label boss. The world was watching too. After Mariah's album, everyone was waiting to see if I could pull off another so-called comeback. The success of the project was all on me, but working with producers of Jimmy and Terry's stature, and an artist of Janet's level, I couldn't call all the shots. They'd each have their say.

Not least I was all nervous about how it would affect my relationship with Janet. I didn't know if we would gel, or if there were gonna be arguments. I didn't even want to walk down that path with her, because we were so tight. I never wanted the business part to get between us. I can be a badass in the studio sometimes. If I don't like something, I don't tell people nicely. How would she take it?

It was all cool. There was some tiptoeing at first, but we all vibed together like we needed to. We were all fans of each other from the get-go. Me and Jan rarely disagreed. I'd suggest something, and she'd either take it or come back with an idea that was better. She also gets her grind on. You have to drag her out of the studio because she'll work way past when she's tired. I always like working with artists who love to work hard.

It was the longest time I ever spent on a single album. I produced seven out of the 11 songs, but because there were other people involved, I had to find a new way of working and make enough room for them. My man Johnta also stepped in on some songs. Instead of just doing each of our tracks separately, we decided to collaborate all the way through to keep the album more consistent.

We'd get all our thoughts and ideas out on the table, then talk about which ones worked and which ones didn't. On one song, I remembered one of Jimmy and Terry's old-school tracks and ran into the studio. Jimmy started playing the song and it gave me an idea.

"You know what, we should do something along these lines as a bass," I said.

They understood me, and I understood them. We had the same music vocabulary. But between SouthSide in Atlanta and Jimmy and Terry's Flyte Tyme studios in L.A., that kind of teamwork takes a minute. We started the work in November 2005 and the album didn't come out until September 2006.

The album wasn't a smash. It debuted at number two on the *Billboard* chart that first week with almost 300,000 units sold, then it sank. I'm proud of that album. Musically we achieved what we set out to achieve. I wanted Jan to get back to her R&B roots and reconnect with her urban base. Times have changed since she and Michael were out in the eighties. Urban artists don't have to do pop records to cross over anymore.

I brought the ghetto and mixed it with echoes of vintage Janet from her *Control* and *Rhythm Nation* days. Catchy dance grooves were put together with some Southern bounce and snap music to connect her with what's going on in the streets today. Some reviews of the album appreciated this. From the Associated Press to *The New York Times*, the real music critics got with what I was trying to do.

But like I said, when you produce an album, the quality of the music is only a part of it. The album itself is only the blueprint. For it to really sell it's up to the record label to package it and do it up right, something that's never been a strength of Virgin. The first single, "Call on Me" featuring Nelly, went to number one.

Jan made sure she did her part. It's part of the Jackson family DNA. For months she trained up to do full-blown performances with a bunch of dancers. Kids these days aren't used to seeing real performances like that. They only know younger artists who don't know nothin' about putting on a good show.

She doesn't always love doing interviews, and she hates answering the inevitable questions about the Super Bowl and her brother. But she did the obligatory red carpeting and opened up to the media like the pro she is. Not that it's always easy to get the press to focus on the music. Backstage at the ESPN award show we were telling reporters about the album's release date and someone asked, "When are you two gonna get married?"

I gave him the most sarcastic answer I could think of:

"On September twenty-six, when the album comes out. Yeah, that's gonna be our wedding day."

The media jumped all over it. It was in the news for weeks. It even made the *Hindustan Times* in India! We all thought it was obvious I was just answering a dumbass question with a joke. But that's the press these days. You tell them the most ridiculous thing, and that's what they print. For a second I forgot what happens when you don't use the power of the dark force wisely!

The idea we had was to make her album release an international event. But getting everyone at the label to be on the same page was harder than making the album itself. I was getting ready to turn into Darth Vader and slice some people with my light saber. I wanted to fire a few asses. They couldn't understand that when you do a contest for fans to choose an album cover you don't just do it in America and exclude the rest of the world, especially not with an artist like Janet. It's like someone has to explain to them what the Internet is.

The label politics coming off of the Janet project was eating up so much of my time that could have been spent in the studio working on other records. Everyone wanted a piece of me. I couldn't give everyone the attention they needed and some of my other artists were starting to get jealous. I didn't see the value added of being part of a major label when I was cranking out music without the support of a big marketing and promotion machine behind me. All those other records I put out for them could have been much bigger if they did what other labels did and actually worked. My side projects for other labels, like the Chingy joint, had a better reaction because they had that backup. But at Virgin I was out there by myself banging my head against a brick wall. It was giving me a headache.

There were so many lil' moments of frustration with Virgin all the way down the line. I knew what would happen way back in October 2005, when the new guy took over. From my first meeting with him I could tell he'd be going in a different direction and my open lane would be cut off. I could predict the future 12 months ahead.

The whole reason I agreed to join Virgin in the first place was because they promised me a free reign in urban music. There were no problems in my department when the CEO took over but he just couldn't leave it alone. Without even discussing it with me he started fiddling, so I knew immediately we were gonna bump heads.

He never put out an urban record before, and here he had one of the biggest urban pop stars in the world working on something. He just had to put his hands on it and take over when he should have been trying to learn what Jermaine Dupri was all about. I could have taught him all he needed to know about my music, but he didn't want to ask. I wouldn't tell him how to put out a Kid Rock album. That's his thing. I was just looking for the same kind of respect.

People assume I left Virgin because of the Janet album, but that was only one piece in a whole pile of things I wasn't happy about. The Virgin executives should have been finding ways to cheerlead and make it happen. Lyor Cohen and Kevin Liles were so successful at Def Jam because they knew to champion what the kids in the street were doing and sell it to people who didn't know. Whatever Irv Gotti or Jay-Z made, they stepped up and sold it for them. That's the beauty of Def Jam.

They give you the title president but it doesn't mean any-thing if there's still someone above you and they don't have your back. It was that whole Anakin situation all over again. A guy like me ends up dividing the building. I'm the younger person in charge who knows just as much as the older guys. I make too much noise. The fact that people were marching to this kid's drum was creating too much tension. The Janet album was my final breaking point. I'm not a person who has to do anything I don't want to do. I don't just go for anything. I work too hard to stand there and watch people tear down everything I build. That's why I decided to quit.

By now you've already heard what my next move was. As I write these last lines I already have a pretty good idea about what's gonna happen. I'm getting ready to put on that Darth Vader mask. I'm about to grow even stronger by joining forces with the giants. The music business is just like running in a race. You put your shorts on and you keep moving forward, fast. All things being equal, it's the young guy who leaves the older, weaker guys in suits behind in the dust. Watch this space to find out who wins.

I'm not saying I haven't had my moments of doubt. The way things went down at Virgin was a huge disappointment to me. The fact that people were dismissing all our hard work on Jan's album as a "flop" hurt me. Those people probably didn't even listen to the music. It was enough for them to know that me and Jan are two successful people who, together, are even stronger. That's enough to make people wait in the wings and pray that you fail. The past two years have been so stressful there were times I had to ask myself, "Is it worth it?"

Then something happened. Last fall, a week before my birthday, the Georgia Music Hall of Fame inducted me as their youngest member. My whole family: my mother, my father, my So So Def kids, my assistants Tyrone and Joshlyn, Diane, my best friend Eddie, and almost everyone who mattered most to me in the world, were in the audience.

I was introduced by Quincy Jones and Russell Simmons, two of my greatest inspirations of all time. On my right was Quincy, the man whose record for producing the best-selling album in history remains untouched. If you're a producer and you don't look up to him I don't know what you're doing in the music business. Quincy called me his baby brother, like he always does, and said I'd still be making history when I turn 80!

On my left was Russell, the first person who ever caught my attention as an entrepreneur. He was the one I saw taking hip-hop to the next level as a business. As someone in our culture who's had so much success running his own companies, Russell gave me the idea early on to do the same. I've looked up to him since I was 12 years old. Russell told the audience *I* was his inspiration, ever since the first days we met on the Fresh Fest tour! If I can combine half the achievements of both of these guys, I'll know I've reached my goal.

The achievement of being the youngest single individual ever to be inducted into the Georgia Music Hall of Fame, being able to set that record with all the music coming out of Atlanta, was a thrill. That's all I ever wanted: to be recognized on my own turf for having started at such a young age. How long is it going to take for somebody else to break that record? The honor meant more to me than any Grammy or hit record could. All the crazy headlines and backstabbing label business didn't matter. This was my moment.

Yeah, it's worth it.

# LAST WORD

*I was lookin' at my life and said I should have a book*
*Somethin' inspirational for anybody that's dreamin' of havin'*
*the same look*
*But as I thought more I realized I didn't have an ending*
*'Cause every time I do something it's back to the beginning*
*People be talkin' like "I know he did that but what's his next*
*move?"*
*So I started questioning if me havin' a book was my best*
*move*
*Then I thought a lil' harder and asked myself, "When have I*
*not taken a chance?"*
*And, "What's the difference in me writing a book*
*And makin' people dance?"*
*NOTHING!!!!!!*

*J.D., 2006*

# ACKNOWLEDGMENTS

A big shout out to y'all who helped me with this book. With so much going on in my life at any given time, it wasn't always easy to remember every detail and pivotal moment in my life and career. I am extremely grateful to all my friends, family, artists, and associates for taking the trouble to jog my memory with their conversations and recollections. Y'all know who you are, an' whatchu mean to me.

—J.D.

# DISCOGRAPHY/CAREER HIGHLIGHTS

- 2005 ASCAP Pop Music Awards/Golden Note Award
- 1999, 2001, 2005 and 2006 ASCAP Rhythm & Soul Awards/ Songwriter of the Year
- 2006 BET Hip-Hop Awards/Element Award: Producer of the Year
- 2006 Billboard R&B/Hip-Hop Awards/Otis Redding Excellence Award, Top Songwriter & Top Producer
- 2006 Georgia Music Hall of Fame/Songwriter Inductee
- 2007 Grammy Nomination for Best R&B Song "Don't Forget About Us"
- 2006 Grammy Award for Best R&B Song Mariah Carey "We Belong Together"

- 2006 Grammy Nomination for work on Mariah Carey Record of the Year, Song of the Year, Album of the Year
- 2005 Grammy Nomination for work on Usher Best R&B Songs "Burn" & "My Boo" and Album of the Year
- 1999 Grammy Nomination for Best Rap Performance by Duo or Group JD & Jay-Z "Money Ain't a Thang"
- 1999 Grammy Nomination for Best Rap Album Jermaine Dupri *Life in 1472*
- 2002 NARAS Atlanta Chapter/Heroes Award
- 2004 EMI Music Publishing/Triple Threat Award
- 2005 Impact/Music Executive of the Year Award
- 2006 Songs of Hope IV/Music Innovator Award
- 2006 NAACP Image Award Nomination for Best Song Mariah Carey "We Belong Together"
- 2006 Lilli Claire Foundation/Music of the Heart Award

## OTHER ACCOMPLISHMENTS

- 2002–03 NARAS Atlanta Chapter President
- 2001 Artists Against AIDS "What's Going On"
- TV & Radio Ads/Heineken Jet Bet feat. JD & Lil Jon, Sprite Remix feat. Craig Mack, Mountain Dew feat. Brat, Sprite feat. Kris Kross
- Video Game Soundtracks/Madden 2000 feat. Ludacris, NBA Live 2004 feat. JD, NBA2K feat. R.O.C.
- Acting appearance in *In Too Deep, Carmen: A Hip Hopera, The New Guy, Moesha* & *A Different World*

## SO SO DEF LABEL RELEASES/EXECUTIVE PRODUCER

- Anthony Hamilton
- Da Brat
- Bone Crusher
- Bow Wow
- Dem Franchize Boyz
- J-Kwon
- Jermaine Dupri
- Jermaine Dupri Presents: *Young, Fly & Flashy Vol. I*, Featuring JD "Gotta Getcha"
- Jagged Edge
- Johnta Austin
- So So Def Bass All-Stars Vol. I–III, Featuring Ghostown DJ's "My Boo" & INOJ "Love You Down"
- Soundtracks/*Big Momma's House, Hardball & Like Mike*
- Xscape
- YoungBloodz

## PRODUCER/SONGWRITER

- Mary J. Blige "Everything" So So Def Remix
- Bow Wow/"Bounce With Me," "Let Me Hold You," "Like You" feat. Ciara, "Shorty Like Mine" feat. Chris Brown & "Fresh AZIMIZ"
- Mariah Carey/"Always Be My Baby," "We Belong Together," "Don't Forget About Us" & "Shake It Off"
- Chingy/"Pullin' Me Back," "Dem Jeans" & "Right Thurr" So So Def Remix

- Da Brat/"Funkdafied," "Give It To You," "Fa All Y'all," "Da B Side" & "That's What I'm Looking For"
- Destiny's Child/"With Me Pt. II"
- Dru Hill/"In My Bed" So So Def Remix feat. JD and Da Brat
- Fantasia/"Got Me Waiting"
- Aretha Franklin/"Here We Go Again"
- Jagged Edge/"Where The Party At," "Gotta Be," "Promise," & "Let's Get Married"
- Janet Jackson/"Someone To Call My Lover" Remix, "Call On Me," & "So Excited"
- Alicia Keys/"Girlfriend"
- Kris Kross/"Jump," "Warm It Up" & "Da Bomb"
- Murphy Lee/"What Da Hook Gon Be"
- LL Cool J/"Control Myself"
- Ludacris/"Get Off Me"
- Monica/"The First Night," "U Should've Known Better" & "Beat Drop"
- MC Lyte/"Keep On, Keepin' On"
- Nelly/"Grillz"
- Kelly Price/"Secret Love" So So Def Remix feat. JD & Da Brat
- Run-DMC/"Can I Get A Witness," "Let's Stay Together," & "It's Over"
- TLC/"My Life," "Kick Your Game," "Switch" & "Bad By Myself"

- Usher/"U Got It Bad," "Confessions, Pt. 2," "My Boo," "Burn," "U Make Me Wanna," "Nice & Slow" & "My Way"
- Xscape/"Just Kickin' It," "Understanding," "Who Can I Run To," "Feels So Good" & "My Little Secret"

## ARTIST

- *Life in 1472*/"Money Ain't a Thang" feat. Jay-Z, "Sweetheart" feat. Mariah Carey
- *Instructions*/"Welcome To Atlanta" feat. Ludacris